in his own words

MORRISSEY

John Robertson

Omnibus Press
London/New York/Sydney/Cologne

Edited by Chris Charlesworth
Art Direction by Mike Bell
Book Designed by Ranch Associates
Picture Research by Debbie Dorman
Project and typesetting co-ordinated by Caroline Watson

ISBN 0.7119.1547.4
Order No: OP44874

Exclusive distributors:
Book Sales Limited
8/9 Frith Street,
London W1V 5TZ, UK
Music Sales Corporation
24 East 22nd Street,
New York, NY 10010, USA
Music Sales Pty. Limited
120 Rothschild Avenue,
Rosebery, NSW 2018, Australia
To the Music Trade only:
Music Sales Limited,
8/9 Frith Street,
London W1V 5TZ, UK

Typeset by Capital Setters, London

Printed in England by Anchor Brendon Press, Tiptree, Essex

Picture Credits

Peter Anderson: p20, 32, 54, 70, 82, 87(B) Andrew Catlin: p5, 6, 12, 16 Kevin Cummins: Front
Cover, p17, 25 Joelle Depont: p94(T) Hulton Picture Library: p44, 74, 77, 79(T) London Features
Int.: p8, 33, 37, 40, 47, 48, 49, 61, 65, 66, 67, 69, 73, 76, 78, 79, (C&B), 80(B), 81, 86, 88, 89, 94(B)
Jo Novark: p10, 19, 27, 29, 35, 58, 59, 62, 63, 91, 95 Network Photographers: p52 Pictorial Press:
p49 Rough Trade: p7, 11, 71, 93 Tom Sheehan: p13, 18, 23, 38, 43, 45, 50, 51, 53, 55, 83, 87(T), 92
Paul Slattery: p14, 15, 28, 30, 31, 57, 85, 96

Every effort has been made to trace the copyright holders of the photographs in this book but one or
two were unreachable. We would be grateful if the photographers concerned would contact us.

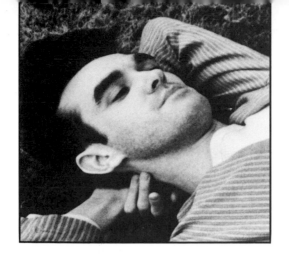

Morrissey is a contradiction. The arch recluse who relishes the media spotlight. The depressive who prances joyously on *Top Of The Pops*. The leader of the archetypal indie band, who signed with EMI. The pacifist who advocated the assassination of Margaret Thatcher. The traditionalist who adopted modern technology. The outsider who became the establishment.

Then there are the rumours, most of which couldn't be mentioned here without fear of a libel suit. And the questions: is Morrissey gay? Is he celibate? Is he a manic depressive, forever close to taking his own life? Or is he laughing up his sleeve, as he notches up another triumph in the Great Rock 'n' Roll Swindle, take two?

'This Charming Man' announced a new rock voice, an individualist who used the clichés of the past to subvert the future. The Smiths promised an end to media puppetry and image mongering; while Johnny Marr soon forgot this pledge and started auditioning for a lead role in 'The Keith Richards Story', Morrissey resolved to avoid the trappings of stardom, the distance that divides us in the stalls from the gods on the stage. And, of course, he duly became a star.

Worse than a star in fact: Morrissey was a role model for every tortured adolescent in a gloomy bedsit. Previous rock depressives had earned their misery, by misuse of love or drugs, or by confusing the two. Morrissey was less glamorous, the ugly boy next door no girl or boy would kiss, the misunderstood genius to whom no one would listen, the artist who had no choice but to suffer.

Just as quickly, The Smiths themselves became a model for a generation or two of young bands, who believed that a combination of worn-out Byrds riffs and a hasty declaration of anguish would make them superstars as well. Radio One's evening shows have been a haven for such meanderings for almost five years; no one seems to have realised that the point was to be individual, not to copy someone else who was. No matter: The Smiths became the most influential British rock group of the eighties, almost despite themselves, whereupon they fell apart.

Morrissey then went solo, making records that substituted synths for Johnny Marr's guitar, but otherwise continued his celebration of English tradition

and adolescent suffering. And still there was the conundrum: a remarkable interview with Paul Morley in *Blitz* revealed a soul in torment, closer to the edge than ever before. The next week, there was the pop star, lapping up the adoration of his fans without a trace of irony. Something was false: but the jury cannot reach a verdict.

Along the way, Morrissey has talked, creating friends and enemies among his pop contemporaries, scandalising the gutter press with talk of violence, sex and hate, and explaining his art in a whirlwind of verbiage that obscures as much as it reveals. More than any star since John Lennon, in his relentless quest for honesty, stopped short of describing his sexual failings and social disasters.

Yet just as Albert Goldman has seen Lennon's soul-baring as a smoke-screen, so there is the possibility that all Morrissey's self-examination and stripping of barriers has itself been a clever game, a conscious attempt to concoct an image which would sell. Here, in his own words on sex, politics, music, childhood, solitude and regret, Morrissey occasionally contradicts himself, like any decent man. But is his every word itself a contradiction? Make up your own minds.

SEX

To me, Ryman's is like a sweetshop. I go in there for hours, smelling the envelopes. I can get terribly erotic about blotting paper, so for me going to Ryman's is the most extreme sexual experience one could ever have.

1985

It's crucial to what we're doing that we're not looking at things from a male stance. I can't recognise gender. I want to produce music that transcends boundaries. SEPTEMBER 1983

The gay connotations could well be harmful when it comes to dealing with the press – I'm sure they could find something dubious in all lyrics. I simply can't get down to gender – I don't mind who listens. I wouldn't like to be thought of as a gay spokesman, though, because it's just not true. NOVEMBER 1983

I think a sex symbol is possibly the best thing to be. NOVEMBER 1983

Are you celibate?

Factually, yes. But I'm open to ideas! I've never been terribly interested in sex in itself. In your formative years you're led to believe lots of magical things will happen with other people – which doesn't actually happen. But then everything we do is just a distraction from reality. NOVEMBER 1983

I hate this 'festive faggot' thing which seems to come through in my interviews, because people listen to 'This Charming Man' and think no further than anyone would presume. I hate that angle, and it's surprising that the gay press have harped on that more than anyone else.

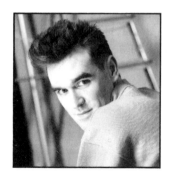

I hate it when people talk to me about sex in a very trivial way, because I can't talk about it in a trivial way, and I think the images we thrust forth are really quite serious and important, and when people simply debase them because they can't be bothered to think about things clearly, when they have this very juvenile, street-level approach to sex, I can't see why they even listen to our music. FEBRUARY 1984

I've always found it (sex) particularly unenjoyable. But that again is something that's totally associated with my past and the particular views I have. I wouldn't stand on a box and say, 'Look, this is the way to do it, break off the relationship at once.' But for me it was the right decision. And it's one that I stand by and I'm not ashamed or embarrassed by. It was simply provoked by a series of very blunt and thankfully brief and horrendous experiences that made me decide upon abstaining, and it seemed quite an easy and natural decision. MARCH 1984

Sex is what most people are motivated by, whether they're involved with it or not. JUNE 1984

The sexes have been too easily defined. People are so rigidly locked into these two little categories. I don't know anybody who is absolutely, exclusively heterosexual. It limits people's potential in so many areas. I think we should slap down these barriers. JUNE 1984

After seven years of celibacy, would a new relationship have to be sexless?

Not at all. It's a long time, but I'm quite prepared to break the record! Celibacy medallions don't interest me, I'm not after a specially inscribed trophy. SUMMER 1984

I think I did have a crush (when I was a teenager) . . . but nothing I was about to put into practice in any way. It was always these very dark desires I had, mostly with people on television which is utterly pointless anyway. But in the real world – well, I just wasn't really there. I never snogged on the corner, if that's what you mean. NOVEMBER 1984

Are you still celibate?

Regrettably, yes! But it was never a platform. I was never out to create a massive movement throughout Britain of mad celibates. You can go out and get casual sex, but that's of no human value. It either happens or it doesn't. For most people relationships are quite unavoidable, although I've managed quite well. NOVEMBER 1984

Is sex overrated?

I honestly don't know. You might be able to say that if you've been frolicking about for years on end. But I think my attitude is quite challenging because it's not really happened before, except with Cliff Richard and he doesn't count. It seems impossible for a public figure in 1984 to be celibate so people find it quite challenging. You know, the whole idea of the pop star bathed in sexuality, yawning at the next round of orgies. NOVEMBER 1984

I think the mission of most journalists is to expose me, because they have this notion that I'm totally fake – as though I'm secretly some mad sex monster. People are ready, in wait, for the cloak to drop and to see me photographed in the Playboy Club. They're trying to unravel me. DECEMBER 1984

As far as sexuality is concerned, I do feel very strongly about it. Therefore I have a very non-sexual stance, seeing people as humanist. There's so much segregation in modern life, the last thing we need is a massive chasm between the sexes, which gets wider as the years pass.

All the so-called liberators spout excessive hatred. On the one side, feminists scream men are the enemies, they're killing us; on the other extreme, it's the Tetley bitter men machismo thing. I refuse to recognise the terms hetero-, bi- and homo-sexual. Everybody has exactly the same sexual needs. People are just sexual, the prefix is immaterial. DECEMBER 1984

On the subject of sex, virtually all the American coverage we've had has been totally erroneous. **DECEMBER 1984**

You couldn't have a world free from sex, that would be impossible. I'd like to cleanse the world of sexual stereotypes, though, because they can be extremely dangerous. It would be quite easy to do if you had control over the media and the images it presents. **JANUARY 1984**

I don't have a love life, but I'm open to ideas. **1984**

I do find many things erotic. As a child of the sixties, when the seats of cars were made of leather, to me there was something highly erotic about actually being in a car. I have always found cars highly erotic – not the driver's seat, there was just something about the old leather seats. **APRIL 1985**

The things that I find erotic are certain situations. They don't even have to be particularly sexual. The erotic feelings I have are very conventional, I'm afraid. It's just – oh, I can't say! It's silly! **APRIL 1985**

One has to protect oneself from eroticism. **APRIL 1985**

I don't want to sleep with anyone any more, I don't want to. I don't. No, I'm not going to instigate things any more. APRIL 1985

The whole idea of womanhood is something that to me is largely unexplored. I'm realising things about women that I never realised before, and 'Some Girls' is just taking it down to the basic absurdity of recognising the contours to one's body. The fact that I've scuttled through 26 years of life without ever noticing that the contours of the body are different is an outrageous farce. JUNE 1986

Are you STILL celibate?

I lapsed slightly; I was caught off guard, as it were. But I return of course as triumphant as ever to the most implausible, unbelievable necessary absurd situation that could ever befall any intelligent person. JUNE 1986

Personally, I have nothing to do with sex, nothing whatsoever. I'm not a tremendous authority on sexuality in general. SEPTEMBER 1986

I'm just dramatically, supernaturally non-sexual. SEPTEMBER 1986

I would like eventually to turn into Germaine Greer. SEPTEMBER 1986

Sex is a waste of batteries. SEPTEMBER 1986

Don't ask me about masturbation. SEPTEMBER 1986

Is celibacy really a victory of guilt over lust?

I wish it was, I wouldn't feel so badly about it then. In fact, I wish it had any purpose whatsoever. It certainly wasn't something I ever tried to instil in the public at large – I never expected a massive movement of celibates storming down Whitehall – it was just something that slipped out, really, in a manner of speaking. It's just the way I choose to live and the way I've always lived. I can't even recommend it. It's just right for me and wrong for the rest of the population. SEPTEMBER 1987

Is there any sex in Morrissey?

None whatsoever. Which in itself is quite sexy. It was never there. It goes back to being an incredibly unpopular person. No one asked. APRIL 1988

Did you ever ask anybody?

Once or twice. Girls and boys. I sent notes. After a while I thought, that is it, that is the end of the notes. I don't want to go through that any more. In a particular sense, I am a virgin. Well, in a very thorough sense, actually! But perhaps if there had been sex, I wouldn't have written. APRIL 1988

I have always expected some fictitious *Sun* spread like, 'Morrissey injects sleeping nun with cocaine', but there's really nothing to report, and I'm half humiliated to have to confess such a thing. FEBRUARY 1988

FANS

I want people who hear us to feel charming and handsome. The disciples we've accumulated are incredibly charming people. They don't spit or gob, they bring flowers.

NOVEMBER 1983

People are dedicated to us because we deserve it. We try. Our reception hasn't surprised me at all. In fact, I think it will snowball even more dramatically over the immediate months – it really has to. I feel very comfortable about it and I'm very pleased. It's all quite natural because I really think we merit a great deal of attention. **NOVEMBER 1983**

Nothing in the past is important really. I was alive, that's all. If people really like The Smiths – and we do have our disciples – I don't think they're interested in whether I had a job once or Johnny owned a caravan. **SEPTEMBER 1983**

We want our audience to be as large as possible. There's no point in having very strong views and hiding them away. You have to reach as many people as possible – to stretch your abilities as far as they can go. It's constantly construed that our attitude about this embodies some kind of outright arrogance, but there's no sense in being sheepish and po-faced. **FEBRUARY 1984**

So many popular groups have seen having a big audience as some kind of stain. The auditorium bit is still linked with so many unwanted faces from the sixties, but I think it's there to be grabbed and utilised. **FEBRUARY 1984**

What kind of fans do the Smiths attract?

Hopefully, all different sorts of people – a real mixture. I've been pleased to see an assortment of age groups at our recent concerts. Married couples, teenagers, mums and daughters. We're really trying to attract the shy sort of person who never goes to gigs, never buys records. Believe it or not, I was like that before I joined the Smiths! **SEPTEMBER 1984**

I get terribly embarrassed when I meet Smiths apostles – I hate the word fans. They seem to expect so much of me. Many of them see me as some kind of religious character who can solve all their problems with a wave of a syllable. It's daunting.
The other night we all went to the Hacienda, and for the entire night I was simply sandwiched between all these Smiths apostles telling me about their problems and what they should do to cleanse themselves of improprieties.
I don't always have the answers for everyone else's lives. It's quite sad to study the letters I receive, and I receive a huge amount of mail every day, vast volumes on people's lives: 'Only you can help me, and if you don't reply to this letter I'll drown.' **NOVEMBER 1984**

Communication with an audience is not a thing you can buy. If you try and it's not there, an audience can spot fakes really easily. **MAY 1983**

When I meet people like this (fans with problems) I start to stumble with words and certainly in a night club situation it's almost impossible to say the most basic things clearly. Lots of people march away thinking I'm a totally empty-headed sieve because I haven't said, 'Go forth and multiply', or something. But if people saw me otherwise, as the hard-assed rock 'n' roller, then I'd just go to bed and stay there. **NOVEMBER 1984**

As a direct result of my attitude to relationships, our audience is split sexually evenly. That's something that pleases me to a mammoth degree. I'd hate it if we excluded 50 per cent of the human race. That is why I feel sad about groups like Bronski Beat who are so steeped in maleness, and quite immediately ostracise 50 per cent of the human race. **NOVEMBER 1984**

You get all these letters from people saying, 'If you don't write back I'm going to commit suicide'?

Yes, it's difficult. We can snigger about it, but it's very difficult because it happens every day and what does one do? if you reply to these letters you become immediately involved and you become absolutely responsible which is a terrible thing. It's sad to me that so many people do think about suicide and so many people's lives are in a shambolic mess, but here we are. **MARCH 1985**

Touring's interesting because it's fascinating to meet people. That sounds silly, but unless we actually tour we don't actually meet the people who buy our records. Which is strange. You can have a hit record and loads of people can buy your records, but you don't actually meet them. And I never meet Smiths apostles ever – so it's only by touring that I can actually come face to face with these people. **MARCH 1985**

SELF

In reality, I'm really all of those very boring things — shy, and retiring. But when one is questioned about the group, one becomes terribly, terribly defensive and almost loud. But in daily life, I'm almost too retiring for comfort.

MARCH 1984

I remember for a long time feeling totally charmless and unhand-some and I know there are many others who feel the same way. It's time that all those people moved in on this whole shebang and if necessary pretend to have charm. For too long this sphere of entertainment has been dominated by the big mouths and the small minds. **NOVEMBER 1983**

Are you an egotist?

It's not really ego. If you have something and you know that you're good, why be shy and hide behind the curtains? There's no point. **SEPTEMBER 1983**

Do you worry about old age? o

That's a long time off and something I don't think about. But age shouldn't affect you. It's just like the size of your shoes – they don't determine how you live your life. You're either marvellous or you're boring, regardless of your age. And I'm sure you know what we are! **SEPTEMBER 1983**

In ordinary situations I cannot survive. I can't have a daily job. I can't be out of my bed by eight o'clock. I can't converse politely with the man next door. But situations that are considered quite surreal I find intensely natural – appearing on TV, touring – they're nice things to do, glamorous. **NOVEMBER 1983**

As my education virtually amounted to nothing – we were instilled with the fact that everything was hopeless – I completely immersed myself in films. Those people replaced the friends I never had. **NOVEMBER 1983**

People thought I was absolutely fake because I really tried to think about things in a manner which didn't seem to appeal to the average person. It's just like the brow-beaten artist, really. **FEBRUARY 1984**

I'm very interested in the idea of being alone, and people feeling isolated – which is the way I think most people feel at the end of the day. I think it's a general condition under which people live, and I often feel that it has something to do with death. Because one is ultimately alone when one dies. **MARCH 1984**

I just live a terribly solitary life, without any human beings involved whatsoever. And that to me is almost a perfect situation. I don't know why, exactly, I'm just terribly selfish, I suppose. Privacy to me is like the old life support machine. I really hate mounds of people, simply bounding into the room and taking over. So when the work is finished, I just bolt the door and draw the blinds and dive under the bed. **MARCH 1984**

Do you like your voice?

Because I'm interviewed so much and in so many ways I'm almost always asked the same questions. When these things emerge in print it constantly seems as though I'm saying the same things all the time, and I could quite imagine that boring people to death very quickly. MARCH 1984

I can't see any benefit whatsoever in being absolutely mute or really having nothing to say or having no opinions whatsoever. And regardless of what one says, there will always be someone standing there in the shadows ready to point and sneer and spit. And you could say something that would appeal enormously to one person, but another person would see it as absolutely hysterical buffoonery. I'm not going to worry too much, because there doesn't seem to be a great deal of point. I feel quite comfortable, really, with the way things are, and I still have the same degree of confidence in the future. Nothing's changed. MARCH 1984

I think it's very attractive. I haven't discovered the things I can't do yet, though I don't think it's suited to certain kinds of opera. NOVEMBER 1984

Without glasses or contact lenses, I'm paralysed. Being immersed in books for years and years, your eyes deteriorate. By the time I was 14, I couldn't see. I've acquired contact lenses in the past few months, they've been a strange rebirth for me. Now I think everybody should wear them, whether they need them or not. NOVEMBER 1984

I like yoghurt with orange in it, and almonds on the yoghurt. I don't eat that day and night but it's a favourite. Recently I've developed a passion for Farley's rusks. I've not eaten meat for decades – I find the idea of eating animals quite absurd. I like wine but I can go for months and months without a drink. NOVEMBER 1984

All my shirts have got a character and history. They're very hard to find. I've spent five hours today searching for shirts and got nowhere. They appear in the oddest places. I'll be somewhere like the Co-Op and a shirt will leap out at me in a surreal way. I've recently discovered a women's chain called Evans Outsize which has wonderful shirts. NOVEMBER 1984

I don't trust a living human being. I find most people totally repugnant, so no wonder I have no social life! I'm more protective, but in ways that are considered selfish. Even though it's often good to be selfish, it gets to a point where it's ridiculous, unhealthy. 1984

Because I come from a penniless background – a shack upon a hill – people find it fake that I come bounding down the hill clutching a copy of *De Profundis*. By rights, I should be sitting here talking about Sheffield Wednesday or the length of Jimmy Hill's beard. But I was locked away for years, reading volume after volume. I don't want to talk like Henry VIII, but it's nice to test how elastic vocabulary can be. NOVEMBER 1984

Other people's children bore me, but if one has a child of one's own flesh and blood, one's attitude changes. Lots of little Morrisseys running around could save the world. NOVEMBER 1984

Oh, definitely a day person. I'm in bed before 10pm. I don't read before I go to sleep but I soon dream – which is the same thing. NOVEMBER 1984

I'm a severe critic – severe upon other people. If a person has a hole in their sock, they crumble before me. NOVEMBER 1984

Only people who don't like me accuse me of arrogance. If they don't like you they say you're arrogant. If they do, they say you're wonderfully confident. NOVEMBER 1984

People who dislike the group say that I'm terribly arrogant, but those people don't interest me. I'm really only concerned with people who actually like the group, who never say I'm arrogant. They always say I'm quite confident, which sounds a little more appealing to the ears. But I can't see any reason to be shy about the whole thing. I'm terribly proud of this group. JUNE 1984

There's an hour of every single day, a silent hour, where I pray for another world. But I'm not enduring it. The business side depresses me intensely, but I battle on. I feel I'm having the last laugh. 1984

There's an endless waterfall of things I have to force myself to do. The wine before each gig was a purgatory. 1984

I never ever had money before, so that's quite exciting to me. I've become alarmingly more cynical, although I was half way there anyhow, and I do distrust people more. I feel a lot sadder, to be quite honest, than I did a year ago. Things have become a lot more serious for me. Professionally, I'm absurdly happy. On a personal level, I have no social life, no friends whatsoever. I still get immensely depressed about death and all the other things that have clouded me since I was eight. Nothing's really changed for me, except I'm now totally isolated in a different part of the country. 1984

Are you a day or a night person?

Do you care about people at all?

Yes, I care enormously. I've got dreadfully high standards, though. The things that are important to me now are the same as always. I'm quite intrigued by friendships and I'd like to have some. I think that would be an entrancing experience, friendship. That would be enough. I'm not greedy. **1984**

The friends I used to have imagine they've been replaced and they certainly haven't. They imagine I go down to the laundrette with Marilyn or someone. They simply don't understand that I haven't had time to answer their letters. **1984**

I am very shy, though I wasn't at school, so I don't know why I am now. I imagined I could escape being miserable if I achieved certain things. I achieved them and I was quite possibly more miserable than ever. I never got beyond that first hurdle with making friends. Constantly I'd walk up to people with a note saying, 'I live round the corner, I think you're quite fascinating, please can we have a picnic on the golf course' or something. **1984**

Are you resigned to solitude?

Not really, although I realise certain things are with me for ever. You can't go through what I went through and forget it. No amount of candy floss and money can erase those things. Although the fears and anguishes I had do make some sense now, I'm quite sure-footed. We all have to realise what we are and what we want and what we can do. I've realised that. **1984**

I often feel I don't want to live much longer and, again this will incite guffaws and gasps because it's such a strong thing to say, but if I'm allowed to be honest about it, I don't want to live much longer. There are certain things that enlighten life but there's such a price to pay. I do feel I'd be disappointed if I got to 50; it would show a lack of resolve, or something. **1984**

Are you still shy?

Yes, I think I am. Although I've come out of my shell considerably over the last year, I'm certainly not the life and soul of the party type. I like to sit quietly in the corner and do a lot of listening. My shyness totally disappears when I go on stage, though. I suppose that's why I enjoy live performances so much. **SEPTEMBER 1984**

Why do you sometimes wear a hearing aid?

Some people think it's a kind of sick joke, but the truth is, a fan wrote to me telling me that she was deaf and felt very depressed about her handicap. At that time, we'd released 'What Difference Does It Make', which is all about appearance making no difference to you. I thought it would be a nice gesture to wear the hearing aid on *Top Of The Pops* to show the fan that deafness shouldn't be some sort of stigma that you try to hide. Basically, I was trying to give her a bit of confidence in herself. **SEPTEMBER 1984**

I was terribly embarrassed when I fell off the stage in New York. **NOVEMBER 1984**

The most irritating rumour is that I spend a great deal of time in clubs laughing hysterically with crowds of devoted friends. I mean, I sit in my draughty bedroom in Kensington and I read these things in the most obscure magazines. To me it's really infuriating. I wouldn't mind if it was true! **NOVEMBER 1984**

The other night, I went out for the first time in ages and somebody came up to me and said, 'Do that funny dance you do.' I felt completely repellent – as if I was some character off a situation comedy, some stand-up comic with a woolly hat and a tickling stick. It seems at times like that as though everything has got completely out of hand. **DECEMBER 1984**

I'm beyond embarrassment now. When your 'private' life is magnified in such a way, you know that nothing will happen to make you shirk and shrink. **DECEMBER 1984**

It's strange, because 18 months ago, nobody on the planet had heard that I was alive. Now, to have your cuff-links the subject of massive national concern is quite curious. **DECEMBER 1984**

I never go out to eat. I have an embarrassingly restricted diet – it's literally yoghurts and apples, nothing else. **SEPTEMBER 1984**

I've never had a social life and I don't have one now. Things haven't changed that much. **SEPTEMBER 1984**

I will die for what I say. **MARCH 1985**

I'm not a rock 'n' roll character. I despise drugs, I despise cigarettes, I'm celibate and I live a very serene lifestyle. But I'm also making very strong statements lyrically, and this is very worrying to authoritarian figures. **MARCH 1985**

I look ill, don't I? **JANUARY 1985**

I don't believe in doctors. I believe in self-cure. I've seen very threadbare GPs and I've seen very expensive doctors, and I find they're all relatively useless. **JANUARY 1985**

Physical illness? I've not really had anything. **1985**

I lie a lot – it's really useful. **1985**

I was never happy when I was young so I don't equate growing old with being hysterically unhappy. To me old age doesn't mean doom, despair and defeat. There are lots of people I know in considerably advanced years that I find fascinating. **1985**

Have you ever placed a lonely hearts ad?

Yes. It said, 'I'm dying of loneliness and need to be rescued else I'll sink into obscurity', which I did. I also put that I was mad, ugly, spotty and totally odorous. No reply. **1985**

I'm still too much acquainted with the whole aspect of poverty. I personally work 24 hours of every single day of the week – relentlessly – and the dividends in that area certainly don't pay off. **AUGUST 1985**

I think it would have been an instrumental. **AUGUST 1985**

If you'd written the song 'Reasons To Be Cheerful Part III', what would be in it?

There are many people out there who are Smiths devotees who are quite willing to accept the fact, and expect, that I will be found dangling from some banisters or swinging from the rafters in some darkened church. **AUGUST 1985**

I want to be used. **OCTOBER 1985**

I'm selfish in a positive way. Self-preservation and all that. I do send off money to the Blue Cross, animal refuges, things like that. **1985**

I've got two friends who I've had for years who make records but are not dramatically famous, and I have one friend who makes records and is dramatically famous and I have a friend who made records and was quite famous but isn't making records at the moment. **1985**

About once a year I burst into tears and I just can't stop. I get the impression that I should do it more often but because I don't everything seems to come out at once. Once in 1984 it was a very horrendous plane journey and for some reason the floodgates just opened, as they say, and didn't stop for the rest of the day. On the plane, in the airport, in the hotel, at the soundcheck, I just couldn't stop. **1985**

I really like 3.30 in the afternoon when the sky is overcast and there's thunder and there's rain and you're watching the Monday Matinée and you've got a nice big solid piece of toast in front of you. That to me is life lived to its fullest. **1985**

I don't feel absolutely entirely miserable. I would do if I couldn't do this. **MARCH 1985**

Happiness is eating an ice cream, happiness can be Bernard Manning – it can be . . . an old woman falling off a donkey! **APRIL 1985**

If you've got a grain of intellect you run the risk of making your critics seem dull. So people feel the need to adopt the most violent attitude, even when they like you. So I don't mind too much, I know what's happening. **JUNE 1985**

Because I say I'm a stainless individual, and because I say it so often, so frequently and so loudly, I suppose people really don't have much choice. They have to consume those words somehow. **JUNE 1985**

People think that in some former life I was a debauched rugby player, or that I've got a stream of illegitimate children cluttering up some home on a hillside. **JUNE 1985**

Why do you buy so many photographs of yourself?

I like them. I like to have a lot of photographs on the wall. I want to chronicle everything. People can picture me laying naked in my house, covered in feathers, rubbing these pictures on myself. But that isn't the case. **JUNE 1985**

Are you terribly vain?

Yes, I am vain. If someone punches me in the face and I lose five teeth then I'm going to be upset, make no mistake about that. Yes, it's vanity I care about the way I look, the way I feel and the way I am – and I don't want to apologise about it. **JUNE 1985**

I would never, ever, do anything as vulgar as having fun. **JUNE 1986**

I was ill, and I said I was ill. Nobody had ever said that they were ill before. Within this beautiful sexy syndrome, I popularised NHS spectacles. I didn't popularise the hearing aid, thank God that didn't catch on, but that again was one of my statements. Not a prop, because that sounds like marshmallow shoes or a polka dot suit. I mean I really maintain to this day that even the whole flowers element was remarkably creative, never wacky or stupid. **JUNE 1986**

We can say, yes, Morrissey, that silly old eccentric, but I think it's nice if somebody who is eccentric can break through. Everybody follows the same rules and does exactly what they're told. All modern groups state the unexpected – fluently, but who cares? **JUNE 1986**

Mentally I don't believe I've ever left home. You always think that as life progresses you're going to open different doors. But the shock to me is that you actually don't. But who will accept describing one's life as a really bad dream? **JUNE 1986**

I'm not happy, I'm not. Almost every aspect of human life really quite seriously depresses me. I do feel that all those tags – the depressive, the monotony – all the tags I've dodged or denied are probably absolutely accurate. When you put me next to Five Star and judge the whole thing against the bouncingly moronic attitude that is so useful if one wants a job in the music industry, then yes, I'm a depressive. JUNE 1986

If I wasn't doing this, I don't honestly believe that I would want to live. JUNE 1986

Although it's very hard for many people to accept, I do actually respect suicide because it is having control over one's life. It's the strongest statement anyone can make, and people really aren't strong. Most people as we know lead desperate and hollow lives. JUNE 1986

Have you ever considered suicide?

About 183 times, yes. I think you reach the point where you can no longer think of your parents and the people you'll leave behind. You go beyond that stage and you can only think of yourself. JUNE 1986

My self-view is that I'm more cynical than romantic, and I do appreciate the value of sarcasm. I'm not a jolly character, a life and soul of the party type, and I suppose I asked for the misery tag. I just didn't expect such a generous response! However, I dispute that I'm the Ambassador of Misery. JUNE 1986

I'm still embedded in a fascination for suicide and intensified depression. JUNE 1986

I never walk, as a rule. I'll jump from the cab to the hotel, from the hotel to the taxi. Which is very mundane. I went to see The Bodines the other night. It was just unbearable, I had to leave. It was just a succession of hands, and knees, and legs. OCTOBER 1986

Are you a grim person?

Yes, I suppose I am really. I think it's an attitude that should be encouraged [. . .] No, I don't really think so, but people look at my interviews and regard me as some kind of character from a Dickensian soup kitchen. There are plenty of things that do give me pleasure – although I can't actually think of any at the moment. SEPTEMBER 1987

I've been termed a manic depressive – usually by people who've never met me – but I am capable of looking on the bright side. I just don't do it very often. SEPTEMBER 1987

I have taste, after all, which is why I'm considered out of step with anything that could be regarded as slightly hip. And because I have taste, and don't really blend in with the general colour of 1987, people think I'm some kind of monument from the last century. **SEPTEMBER 1987**

I do have the ability to laugh at myself, even though amongst the people who consider me overwrought this is apparently sinful. I have always had to laugh at myself. If I hadn't found my social position when I was a teenager so amusing, I would have strangled myself. **APRIL 1988**

I have seen one or two psychiatrists. They just sit and nod and doodle. **APRIL 1988**

I do think that I have achieved a great deal as a human being. **APRIL 1988**

I always find when the doorbell rings that my automatic response is to hide or run away, to be quiet. They might want you to do something that you don't want to do, want you to go where you don't want to go. The terrifying thing is, as you get older, it doesn't get any easier. Fears just seem to cement into place. **APRIL 1988**

What was the first song you wrote?

Oh, it was so woeful. It was about bringing flowers to some maiden on a hillside. I was only six, but that's no excuse. **MAY 1984**

I really do mean it when I shower people in flowers. They appreciate the honesty in the act. It was something I felt compelled to do because the whole popular music scene had become so grey and dull I thought something had to be injected, and flowers were just a very sensible injection. **NOVEMBER 1983**

It's not a gimmick. As long as we've been in existence, we've used the flowers, and it's interesting that in recent months quite a few groups have also begun to do exactly what I do. Like Echo and the Bunnymen and Big Country! **SEPTEMBER 1983**

The flowers actually have a significance. When we first began, there was a horrendous sterile cloud over the whole music scene in Manchester. Everybody was anti-human and it was so very cold. The flowers were a very human gesture. They integrated harmony with nature – something people seemed so terribly afraid of. It had got to the point in music where people were really afraid to show how they felt, to show their emotions. I thought that was a shame, and very boring. The flowers offered hope. **SEPTEMBER 1983**

There's a tremendous amount of repression. It was why I intro-duced the flowers on stage – to reduce people's hostility. **NOVEMBER 1983**

How much have you spent on flowers in the past 12 months?

Oh dear, I think it could have kept the DHSS afloat. I don't buy them myself – I've got a flower aide. Now the flowers are written into the contract for each venue and they're provided. They're virtually more important than the PA system. **MARCH 1984**

Why do you wear a bush in your back pocket?

The twigs and things in my back pocket are just a joke. It's just me showing that the music business is completely over the top. There's no need to look for deep, inner meanings – it's just a silly schoolboy prank. **MARCH 1984**

It was the end of a stage for us, and in a way it was parody. But also, to me, it was high art. People laughed at the Pre-Raphaelites, remember that I did think it was quite artistic. For one thing, it had never been done before, and to me it's quite serious. **DECEMBER 1984**

Was appearing on Top Of The Pops with a bush up your backside parodying the popular image of yourself?

People stop me in the street and say, 'Where's your bush?' Which is an embarrassing question at any time of the day. I mean, what do you say to people, 'I've left it behind on the mantelpiece'? But I don't mind if people remember me for my bush – as long as it's for artistic reasons. **DECEMBER 1984**

I will not do the kind of things you're meant to do when you're famous. **APRIL 1988**

PAST

As a child, I was quite deliriously happy. We had no money, but they were naïvely pleasant times. But as a teenager, I could never stress how depressed I was.

JUNE 1984

I had quite a happy childhood until I was six or seven, after that it was horrendous. At the age of eight I became very isolated – we had a lot of family problems at that time – and that tends to orchestrate your life. I had a foul adolescence and a foul teenage existence. Except you couldn't really call it an existence. I just sort of scraped through, escaping into films and books until The Smiths happened and allowed me to live again. **NOVEMBER 1983**

I went through a long, strange period of self-development with words and singing, so I really felt ready when the time came. I didn't feel, 'Good grief, can I do it, can't I do it.' I was just really so desperate to do it that I just did it. When you're really desperate, it's surprising what you can do. **NOVEMBER 1983**

Before I joined the group I was in a serious medical condition. **MAY 1983**

I was very depressed for a very long time previous to The Smiths, simply because I wanted to do it so much. I don't want to go into it, but everything I put into this group now is an extension of what happened to me previously. **SEPTEMBER 1983**

I read persistently. I swam in books as a child, and at some point it becomes quite ruinous. It gets to the point where you can't answer the door without being heavily analytical about it. But ultimately I think they've proved to be positive weapons for me now. I feel that if I hadn't been through that very swamped period, I perhaps couldn't deal with this whole new situation, or The Smiths would be just another group, just hovering along and disappearing quickly. I really and sincerely believe that. **FEBRUARY 1984**

It seemed suddenly that the years were passing, and I was peering out from behind the bedroom curtains. It was the kind of quite dangerous isolation that's totally unhealthy. It was like a volunteered redundancy, in a way. Most of the teenagers that surrounded me, and the things that pleased them and interested them, well, they bored me stiff. It was like saying, 'Yes, I see that this is what all teenagers are supposed to do, but I don't want any part of this kind of drudgery.' **MARCH 1984**

It was like living through the most difficult adolescence imaginable. But all this becomes quite laughable. Because I wasn't handicapped in a traditional way. I didn't have any severe physical disability. I just about survived it, let's just say that. **MARCH 1984**

I lived a hopelessly isolated life. I literally never, ever met people. I wouldn't set foot outside of the house for three weeks on a run. **JUNE 1984**

The power of the written word really stung me, and I was also entirely immersed in popular music. **JUNE 1984**

I never got what I wanted. I was ignored by the whole universe as a child. I spent my entire childhood with my head buried in a pillow, which was . . . quite interesting! **1984**

The realisation that suicide was quite appealing and attractive happened when I was eight. **1984**

I was never young. Periods where, by law, you were meant to be totally reckless, I was absurdly, cripplingly serious. I could never relax, I never accepted my sexuality. This idea of fun: cars, girls, Saturday night, bottle of wine . . . to me, those things are morbid. I was always attracted to people with the same problems as me. It doesn't help when most of them are dead! **1984**

As a child I went to this Catholic school: they fed us this idea of heaven and living for ever and ever and ever. It used to petrify me. Can you imagine living this life without end? It's horrific. **1984**

One has to dwell on the past, and I will never escape, because the past is me. That's exactly what I am. It's insurmountable. **1984**

Will you never escape the past?

I decided that I was going to be a pop star at a very early age, but I wasn't too sure about my capabilities. I sang in the school choir, but that doesn't really count. **SEPTEMBER 1984**

As a teenager, I was intensely shy, so I used only to sing in the bath. One day, I realised I had a voice – but it took me years to pluck up enough courage to let anyone else hear it. **SEPTEMBER 1984**

I often recount tales of total morbidity, but I can't remember the old rolling in the hay bit, out in the countryside sketching horses or whatever. I can simply remember being in very dark streets, penniless. **NOVEMBER 1984**

I'm afraid school was very depressing. It was a very deprived school – total disinterest thrust on the pupils, the absolute belief that when you left you would go down and down and down. It was horrible. A secondary modern school with no facilities, no books, the type of school where one book has to be shared by 79 pupils – that kind of arrangement. **NOVEMBER 1984**

If you dropped a pencil, you'd be beaten to death. It was very aggressive. It seemed that the only activity of the teachers was whipping the pupils, which they managed expertly. There was no question of getting CSEs, for heaven's sake, never mind a degree in science or something. It was just, 'All you boys are hopeless cases so get used to it.' **NOVEMBER 1984**

I never wanted to get off PE – it was the only intellectual subject in school. But I did used to get off all the other subjects. I just used to be constantly ill – general manic depression, mainly. I didn't need notes or anything. They just had to take one look at me and that was enough. **MAY 1984**

Incessantly. It was the only real basis of our relationship. I couldn't think of anything else to do with them. What do they do for a living? Very respectable and interesting jobs, but nothing worthy of being in your illustrious paper. **MAY 1984**

I never had an adolescence. I went straight from six to 46. Quite depressing, really. I missed out on all those things like discos at Christmas. I suppose I've now regressed, but I wouldn't call it a second childhood, because it's my first. **MAY 1984**

Some unwritten law states that you're not supposed to admit to an unhappy childhood. You pretend you had a jolly good time. I never did. I'm not begging for sympathy, but I was struggling for the most basic friendships. I felt totally ugly. **1984**

I was such an intellectual idiot, people were convinced that if they talked to me I'd quote Genesis and bolts of lightning would descend from the sky. So I was never kissed behind the bicycle sheds. **1984**

The 100 metres was my *raison d'être*. I won everything. I was a terrible bore when it came to athletics. **MAY 1984**

I was never bullied at school, I must admit. I was never picked on, never pushed around. It's not very interesting, is it? **MAY 1984**

I started wearing glasses seriously when I was 13. I needed to wear them much sooner, but glasses had this awful thing attached to them that if you wore them you were a horrible green monster and you'd be shot in the middle of the street. So I was forced to wear them at 13 and I've stuck with them ever since. **MAY 1984**

I left home spasmodically and I returned home spasmodically for years. I was never very good at it. I think the first time was when I was 17 and the last when I was 23. I just went to the usual foul, decrepit bedsits that simply crush your imagination. **MAY 1984**

Did you argue with your parents?

I always wanted to be a librarian. To me that seemed like the perfect life: solitude; absolute silence; tall, dark libraries. But then they started to become very modern, you know, these little prefabs, and they had no romance whatsoever. So suddenly the idea had no fascination for me. **MAY 1984**

I hear you're fond of Valium.

Valium? I used to be. As a distraught 15-year-old. **APRIL 1985**

I'm not obsessed with adolescence. It was something, as probably lots of people can gather, I didn't cope with too cleverly. So I do feel bitterness, but I'm not massively, incurably obsessed with it. **MARCH 1985**

Did you ever get beaten by masters at school?

Yes. I wasn't really on the hit list, I wasn't one of those people who were dragged out every single day, but I found that I was certainly in the running for that. I always found I was hit and beaten for totally pointless reasons, which is what I'm sure every pupil would say. But I think in my case I deserve special consideration . . . **JUNE 1985**

The past is so very important. I don't like it when people say, let's leave the past and go ahead, because a lot of the future isn't that attractive. **JUNE 1985**

Who did you blame for
your misery?

I learned that if I ever wanted to be educated I'd have to leave school. So anything I learned was from outside of the education system. I came from a working class background and very brutal schooling, which is of no use to anyone who wants to learn. So education, quite naturally, had no effect on me whatsoever. JUNE 1985

I think I always blamed myself. I always felt, 'These things are happening because I'm an awkward, ugly, gawky individual', and that stayed with me for years and years. I used to believe that if I wasn't successful in any way it was because I was a totally worthless shallow slob. In some totally inexplicable way, I still accept a lot of the blame. Perhaps it isn't right, but I do. Guilt and regret are the most futile emotions in the universe. JUNE 1985

The Catholic church has nothing in common with Christianity. I can remember being at school on Mondays and being asked, 'Did you go to church yesterday?' And if you hadn't been, you literally had the arms twisted off you. It's 'We'll sever your head for your own good, you'll learn my son.' JUNE 1985

It is difficult to describe how insular I was, especially when I was 21, 22, 23. I was entirely on my own. The very idea of me becoming what I have become was unthinkable. I found life unbearable at times. It's very hard when you don't really like people! There should be a union formed to protect us. APRIL 1988

I remember it all in great detail, I seem to remember it every night and re-experience the embarrassment of it. It was horror. The entire school experience, a secondary modern in Stretford called St. Mary's. The horror of it cannot be over-emphasized. Every single day was a nightmare. In every single way you could possibly want to imagine. Worse . . . the total hatred. The fear and anguish of waking up, of having to get dressed, having to walk down the road, having to walk into assembly, having to do those lessons. I'm sure most people at school are very depressed. I seemed to be more depressed than anyone else. I noticed it more. APRIL 1988

Because I had such an intense view about taking one's life, I imagined that this must be my calling, suicide, nothing more spectacular or interesting. I felt that people who eventually took their own lives were not only aware that they would do so in the last hours or weeks or months of their life. They had always been aware of it. They had resigned themselves to suicide many years before they actually did it. In a sense, I had. APRIL 1988

POLITICS

My nightmare is Orwell's vision of 1984, that very mechanical, non-human world.

1984

So many people are sad nowadays because of this pretence that we've advanced into some hi-tech computer age. It's just not true, and computers shouldn't be glorified. Nobody wants a world full of computers, ruled by screens. **NOVEMBER 1983**

You have to be interested in politics these days. If you're not, you're a completely lost individual. Whereas, years ago, politics seemed to be this thing that was secluded for a minority of intellectuals, these days you can't get away with that argument – you have to be attuned to what's happening, there's so much at stake. There's absolutely no excuse for people who aren't politically aware. **NOVEMBER 1983**

I really believe that complacency is bred. It's a recurring theme promoted by a government that says, 'Look, do not worry about nuclear weapons – we will look after you.' Governmental issues aren't translated in a way understandable to most people. Issues are deliberately veiled to prevent people from grasping the point at hand and then forming their own opinion. **NOVEMBER 1983**

This government runs on a bedrock of naïvety. They won't give things away; obviously it's not in their interests. Ultimately people feel it's all beyond them – we want to change that. The Smiths will push people to think for themselves, to believe they can really do something. **NOVEMBER 1983**

There's a certain spirit that people now crave because everybody is depressed. We're moving rapidly into a sphere that nobody wants to go into. Progress doesn't seem to be in any degree pleasant. Everything modern is quite foul. **JUNE 1984**

The entire history of Margaret Thatcher is one of violence and oppression and horror. I think that we must not lie back and cry about it. She's only one person, and she can be destroyed. I just pray there is a Sirhan Sirhan somewhere. It's the only remedy for this country at the moment. **JUNE 1984**

I did say, 'The only thing that could possibly save British politics would be Margaret Thatcher's assassination.' After that I was swamped by telephone calls from the British press asking me what I'd do if a Smiths fan went out and shot Maggie. 'Well,' I said, 'I'd obviously marry this person!' They wouldn't print that. They're not interested in that view. **NOVEMBER 1984**

The sorrow of the Brighton bombing is that Thatcher escaped unscathed. The sorrow is that she's still alive. But I feel relatively happy about it. I think that for once the IRA were accurate in selecting their targets.

Immediately after the event, Maggie was on television attacking the use of bombs – the very person who absolutely believes in the power of bombs. She's the one who insists that they're the only method of communication in world politics. All the *grande dame* gestures about these awful terrorist bombs is absolute theatre. **NOVEMBER 1984**

Will you be taking part in the anti-heroin crusade?

I was asked, but no. I feel quite nervous about it although I adhere to the emotions behind the whole concern. I don't like banners. I think people get into drugs simply because they want to. I don't believe people who say 'I'm trapped, I can't stop this.' It's a lot of bosh really. **NOVEMBER 1984**

I feel so strongly about politics I would like to have some kind of involvement with local politics here in Manchester. I feel so strongly about the way the city is being completely defaced and made uninhabitable. It's so ugly now, vastly ugly. And it reflects itself in the attitudes of the people. I wonder why someone like me cannot get involved with local politics. Why should we leave it to the other slobs? **NOVEMBER 1984**

Times are desperate. The prospect of death is imminent every second of the day. But I think people are more politically attuned now than ever before. I think there's a new political awareness in England now – people want answers. But they're still too lax about everything, I feel. **NOVEMBER 1984**

I'm not totally averse to violence. I think it's quite attractively necessary in some extremes. I would say that violence on behalf of CND is absolutely necessary, because all sorts of communication via peaceful methods are laughed at and treated with absolute violence by the government. Therefore I think it's now time to fight fire with fire and attack very strongly. I don't think that is terrorism, it's more a self-defence. Obviously CND care about the people and that's why they do what they do. That's patriotism. In some cases I think violence is profoundly necessary – when the consequences of no violence are frightening. **DECEMBER 1984**

We don't need all this excessive technology, it's just a select bunch of people who think we have to keep up with the Japanese. People's requirements are quite basic. You need food and shelter but anything else you can live without. **1984**

Margaret Thatcher

The world should be nuclear free. So much is at stake that if we don't get rid of nuclear weapons, we're all in an immense amount of danger. I'd love to be optimistic about the future, and I do have a lot of faith in human spirit, but if Margaret Thatcher did get re-elected . . . **1984**

I think audiences get bored with groups introducing strong hardcore politics into every song. You don't have to be madly blunt in a political sense. To me that lacks a certain degree of intellect. And although we haven't made any abrasively bold statements in a lyrical sense, I think people can gauge where we stand. **DECEMBER 1984**

You need a government to run the country, but people should have control over it and it should work for them. **1984**

Ordinary people don't know their own strength any more. They've been indoctrinated to believe that they're powerless to do anything. **1984**

The common sense for the future is to try and preserve as much as we can from the past. So many new buildings are just modern monstrosities – they offend everyone. **1984**

It seems that ultimately, regardless of what happens in the world, the only way to solve our disagreements is by violence, is by nuclear weapons. And as long as we live in a world where nuclear weapons are the only answer, and the ultimate answer after conversation has failed, I think people will be violent. MARCH 1985

From the time that you get hit when you're a child, violence is the only answer. Conversation is pointless. MARCH 1985

Where do you stand on the Greenham women?

It's a total fiasco. It's failing. They're being kicked about, they're being thrown around, they're being laughed at, they're being shot. I think it should register in their minds that it's not actually working. Something else has to be done. MARCH 1985

Does violence have to be met by violence?

Yes it does. That's the tragedy. That's the massive tragedy of all these issues. It has to be, because of the present government, who can only think in violent terms. MARCH 1985

Personally, I'm an incurably peaceable character. But where does it get you? Nowhere. You have to be violent. MARCH 1985

Do you sympathise with the striking miners?

Completely. Endless sympathy. It's more distressing than most people realise, I think. I think it's the end if they go down, the absolute end. And, of course, it just proves that democracy in this country doesn't exist in any form. MARCH 1985

Did you get any feedback about your comments on the Brighton bombing?

I was hounded from pillar to post. That was the absolute rope around the neck, and I couldn't get away from that. It seemed almost as if I was responsible for the assassination of Thatcher. MARCH 1985

If somebody from the *Daily Mail* comes along and shoots me, that's the way it has to be. I'll die defending what I say. MARCH 1985

Everybody on a public platform is a preacher. But most people preach absolute monotony and it's accepted, and because I like to feel in an absolutely misguided way that I don't, everybody sticks their pins in me. MARCH 1985

On playing a concert for Red Wedge:

Without wishing to sound pugnaciously ponsified, I wasn't terribly impassioned by the gesture. I thought the overall presentation was pretty middle-aged. And I can't really see anything especially useful in Neil Kinnock. I don't feel any alliance with him but if one must vote this is where I feel the black X must go. So that is why we made a very brief, but stormy, appearance. When we took to the stage, the audience reeled back in horror. They took their Walkmans off and threw down their cardigans. Suddenly the place was alight, aflame with passion! JUNE 1986

MANCHESTER

**The whole Gracie Fields, George Formby, Frank
Randall mentality is one I completely worship.
I adore those old Northern troupers and I'd
love to be remembered as following in their
tradition, but it seems doubtful I'll be
remembered at all.**

SEPTEMBER 1987

George Formby

What part have you
played in the Manchester
music scene?

We've had a great deal of personal support from the people at the Hacienda, when they could easily have ignored us for signing with Rough Trade in London rather than Factory in Manchester; and that's good because it means attitudes are at last changing. **NOVEMBER 1983**

I could never be considered a Southerner. I'll always be wandering around the North somewhere. I see Northern qualities dying very quickly and I wish they wouldn't. There's a naïvety and an innocence there that's going. I've always liked the idea of people being humble and getting on with their daily lives. **NOVEMBER 1984**

I certainly don't miss Whalley Range, that would be impossible. I drove through it the other day and it was quite depressing, the whole aura of the place was very repressive, as it always had been, and I felt great sorrow for the people who were still nailed to the place. **NOVEMBER 1984**

I was always there somewhere, lurking in the shadows. It just took me longer to spring forth. I watched the rise of many people as an ominous spectator. Factory and all their groups have been very supportive. We're very popular in Manchester. We've sold out Manchester Free Trade Hall, which I find very gratifying. I suppose there must be something very Mancunian about us. **NOVEMBER 1984**

The way I write is very Northern. I'm not in the least infected by London or the South. **DECEMBER 1984**

In Manchester there's a body of people who are very negative about us, but they're the very ones who, if we disappeared in a blizzard tomorrow, would say, 'Ooh, what a shame.' **JUNE 1985**

I really lived quite fully in Manchester . . . I really scoured the area, and it's very odd for me now to see those places and to have certain tremors of nervousness or excitement or whatever those tremors might be. It just seems like another lifetime. Indeed, it was. **OCTOBER 1986**

In much the same way that people in England might be fascinated by Hollywood, people in America, at least thousands of them I've met, are just enthralled by Manchester. I know absolutely coach–loads of people who come from places like Arizona to see a sign that says 'Whalley Range'. There are people in Houston, Texas, who would burn their mother without hesitation to sit here and look out of that window, and be caught in a thunderstorm. **OCTOBER 1986**

The typical Manchester iciness – nobody really speaks to each other and when they do it's on a really superficial digging nature. **OCTOBER 1986**

The memories I have of being trapped in Piccadilly bus station while waiting for the all−night bus, or being chased across Piccadilly Gardens by some 13−year−old Perry from Collyhurst wielding a Stanley knife. Even when I was on the bus, I would be petrified because I would always be accosted. They were the most vicious people. They would smack you in the mouth and ask you what you were looking at after. **SEPTEMBER 1986**

The frustration that I felt at the age of 20 when I still didn't feel easy walking around the streets on which I'd been born, where all my family had lived. It was a constant confusion to me why I never really felt, 'This is my patch. This is my home. I know these people. I can do what I like, because this is mine.' It never was. I could never walk easily. **SEPTEMBER 1986**

I can remember the worst night of my life with a friend of mine, James Maker, who is lead singer with Raymonde now. We were heading for Devilles. We began at the Thompson's Arms, we left and walked around the corner where there was a car park, just past Chorlton Street bus station. Walking through the car park, I turned around, and suddenly there was a gang of 30 beer monsters, all in their late twenties, all creeping round us. So we ran. Unfortunately, they caught James and kicked him to death, but somehow he managed to stand up and start running. So James and I met in the middle of Piccadilly bus station and tried to get on a bus that would go back to Stretford.

We jumped onto the bus and thought, 'Saved' and turned around – and saw that it was completely empty, no driver. We thought, 'My God. We're trapped on this bus.' They were standing at the door, shouting 'Get out! Get out!' We had all these coins and we just threw them in their faces and flew out of the bus. We ran across the road to a bus going God knows where outside The Milkmaid. We slammed our fares down and ran to the back seat. Suddenly the emergency doors swing open and these tattooed arms fly in – it was like Clockwork Orange.

The bus is packed – nobody gives a damn. So we run upstairs and the bus begins to move and we end up in Lower Broughton. For some reason we get out and we're in the middle of nowhere – just hills.

On top of this hill we could see a light from this manor house. We went up these dark lanes and knocked on the door. It was opened by this old, senile, decrepit Teddy Boy, no younger than 63, with blue suede shoes on. 'Do you have a telephone?' 'No.'

We had to walk back to Manchester. It took us seven days. We came back home to my place, finally, at something like 5am, and listened to 'Horses' by Patti Smith and wept on the bed. That's my youth for you in a nutshell. **SEPTEMBER 1986**

The gay scene in Manchester was a little bit heavy for me. **SEPTEMBER 1986**

I never liked Dale Street. There was something about that area of Manchester that was too dangerous. **SEPTEMBER 1986**

Do you miss living in the North?

I do, but it's just not feasible to stay there at this time in my life. Old ladies still leave presents outside my house in Manchester – cards, fruit, flowers, fluffy toys – all of which are much appreciated. Why do they do it? They want to mother me, I suppose. **SEPTEMBER 1987**

JOHNNY MARR

Johnny can take the most basic, threadbare tune and you'll just cry for hours and hours and swim in the tears.

NOVEMBER 1983

He had really quite simplistic ideals, which at the time was rare, and that was a perfect foundation for what we wanted to do. He also works very quickly, without anxiety, which I like. So many people seem to enjoy talking about things and so few people seem to enjoy doing them. And that's really been the history of the group, that we've got on with things. **FEBRUARY 1984**

Johnny came up and pressed his nose against my window. Quite literally. It left a terrible smudge. I think he'd been eating chocolate or something. He seemed terribly sure of what he wanted to do, which I liked. He said, 'Let's do it and do it now.' So we did it. Then. **FEBRUARY 1984**

How do you relate to the other Smiths?

Very strongly. Let it be said here and now that I'm massively dedicated to them as individuals, to the point of love. Obviously, with Johnny, I feel very defensive about our relationship. Some things have to be shielded, but the dedication I feel for him is quite solid and impregnable. **JUNE 1985**

MEDIA

The tabloids hound me, and it gets very sticky. What makes me more dangerous to them is the fact that I lead somewhat of a religious lifestyle.

MARCH 1985

On allegations that The Smiths condoned child molesting:

We were totally aghast at *The Sun* allegations, and even more so by *Sounds*. We really can't emphasise how much it upset us because obviously it was completely fabricated. I did an interview with a person called Nick Ferrari – and what developed in print was just a total travesty of the actual interview. It couldn't possibly be more diverse in opinion. Quite obviously we don't condone child molesting or anything that vaguely resembles it. What more can be said? **SEPTEMBER 1983**

It's quite laughable coming from a newspaper like *The Sun*, which is so obviously obsessed with every aspect of sex. So it's all really a total travesty of human nature that it's thrown at us, such sensitive and relatively restrained people. I live a life that befits a priest, virtually, and to be splashed about as a child molester – it's all unutterable. **SEPTEMBER 1984**

On our David Jensen session, one song, 'Reel Around The Fountain', was chopped simply because the word 'child' was mentioned and they were frightened people might put the wrong interpretation on it. **SEPTEMBER 1984**

So many people don't talk to the press or appear on TV. You can only presume that it's due to their absolute lack of imagination that they cannot utilise these mediums. You don't have to deface the set or kill the DJ. Just do what you do, and if that isn't enough you shouldn't be here. **FEBRUARY 1984**

I really can't survive being misquoted. And that happens so much, I sit down almost daily and wonder why it happens. But the positive stuff, one always wants to believe, and the insults one always wants not to believe. When one reads of this monster of arrogance, one doesn't want to feel that one is that person. **MARCH 1984**

Television still has this mystical ability to separate you from the world and confer importance on you. I've never understood that. I can't understand people who find it a great joy to send off to Simon Bates and get him to mention their Uncle Bert on the air. **MARCH 1984**

I get really tired of watching groups with bedazzling stage shows and all those wonderful videos in Egypt. **NOVEMBER 1984**

We'll never make a video as long as we live. **NOVEMBER 1984**

I find doing *Top Of The Pops* great fun, which is something that's very hard for the old lips to say. They always give us a semi-royal reception. I know I should spit on the whole idea of *Top Of The*

Pops, but I can't. I think the groups who criticise *Top Of The Pops* are those that probably know they'll never get on there. **NOVEMBER 1984**

All the interviews were becoming completely predictable, because everybody was asking me the same questions. When it appeared in print, it seemed as though I was very boring and that I could only talk about a limited number of things. That wasn't true. I needed to step back, so I've only done one in four months, which for me shows great restraint. **DECEMBER 1984**

I initially gave the impression that I would answer questions on any given subject, regardless of how personal they might be. So people began to probe into the depths of the old soul, as a matter of complete course. Having to go through it several times a day – it's like staring at your own reflection in the mirror for 24 hours in a day, it's quite daunting. It was like constantly being on the psychiatrist's couch, people coming in asking, 'Well, how ill are you today, how miserable are you now', like I was making a miraculous recovery from some great illness. **DECEMBER 1984**

I do read the music press, so it's nice to have that media approval. But it doesn't determine the way I write. I never sit down and say, well, I really have to do this because otherwise such and such a paper won't like me very much. But it is very good to get the support of the music press, I can't deny that. **SEPTEMBER 1984**

I do get the advance chill of a backlash. And it's bang on time. And it's really quite expected. **SEPTEMBER 1984**

In my perfect world I'd definitely have television. I think it's a wonderful invention. Simply because you have one, doesn't mean you have to watch it all the time. It's a very powerful medium, but very educational. It has been abused, but that's more to do with the government than the invention itself. **1984**

It's gone beyond television to video games, which kill children eventually. When I was a child it was almost a mortal sin to be caught indoors – now you can walk through council estates and not see any children. They're all inside glued to their video games – these days, if a child is outdoors it's as if he's gone delirious. As a result children are very monotonous creatures. **1984**

We've avoided video for all our career – and it's paid tremendous dividends, and it's been somewhat of a blot on the face of the industry. I always said that we could become successful without a video and we have done, so the point has been proved. I'm not leading up to saying we're about to make a video – but it would be nice to make some kind of a film, obviously with the height of artistry and skill. **AUGUST 1985**

Journalists, mainly. **MARCH 1985**

What specific targets do you have for your anger?

When we say the word 'entertainment', we think of Leslie Crowther – who's never entertained me – we think of *The Price Is Right*. The things that entertained me in the past always horrified everybody else. **MARCH 1985**

On the controversy about 'Suffer Little Children':

This is the world we live in. It's not a reflection of me, it really reflects the absolute and barbaric attitudes of the daily press. I don't feel that I was in the dock, I feel they were really. In retrospect, they were just really saying how narrow-minded and blunderous they were. Some of the reports in newspapers in Portsmouth and Hartlepool – all the places that really count – some of the reports were so full of hate, it was like I was one of the Moors Murderers, that I'd gone out and murdered these children. It was incredible. **MARCH 1985**

How do you feel about your treatment by the national press?

It's been wonderful and it's been atrocious. It's really impossible for me to have a very clear view of it, so I don't really know. A lot of it has made me really distressed, but it's really only made me distressed because I care so much, which is quite wrong. But I do get distressed about vulgar comments. **MARCH 1985**

I know for a fact 'Shakespeare's Sister' wasn't played on the radio. The record's merits are irrelevant here. With our status it should have automatically had a high profile, but it was blacklisted by the BBC because I denounced the BPI Awards. The sinner must be punished . . . **JUNE 1985**

I thought I was thin enough to take journalism. But I wasn't brutal enough to be a successful journalist, because to be a successful journalist you have to go to Singapore for 10 years and shoot people in the jungle. **OCTOBER 1986**

Of the Derek Jarman videos, 'Panic' was definitely the best. We never actually met Jarman – he did them privately while we were in America, which was absolutely the only way we'd agree to do it. **SEPTEMBER 1987**

Videos are just too time consuming. Videos are just too much of a gigantic distraction from things that are really important. **SEPTEMBER 1987**

They should bury *Coronation Street*. It's silly. The script is beyond credulity. I don't understand it. It's like *Postman Pat*, you know, somebody loses an envelope, somebody breaks an umbrella, and suddenly the credits roll, and there's sad music. And you're expected to be there next week and be worried about the umbrella. **OCTOBER 1986**

I hate the political, the ethical idea of the pop video. I don't like 'promo', I don't like all those words. I'd rather they did not exist. **OCTOBER 1986**

We aren't on TV as much as our status befits, and part of that is deliberate. We get asked on too many programmes we'd rather not do, and too few programmes we'd like to appear on. **SEPTEMBER 1987**

Songs are at least 50 per cent about imagination, and videos crush that element of imagination that's the listener's contribution. What you don't put in, you can't get out. **SEPTEMBER 1987**

My fundamental objection to videos is that everyone who makes them looks so silly. If I thought videos had a chance and there was something salvageable in the whole medium I'd give it a whirl. But videos have the opposite effect on me they're meant to – whenever I see a bad video, I always think, 'Oh no, WHY did they do it? Now I definitely won't buy the record.' **SEPTEMBER 1987**

It's interesting that virtually none of the serious music journalism deals with the Top 30 any more – that's a separate world, one that it seems we're far too intellectual to criticise. By the music press being so detached from that horrible blob, it means that you can't really dig in and change the blob. It just exists and grows bigger and bigger. And attacks people on the street. **OCTOBER 1986**

LOVE

It's largely things rather than people that I do become in love with. I do think it's possible to go through life and never fall in love, or find someone who loves you.

JUNE 1985

Are you removed from love?

I'm physically removed, but there are so many aspects of it. Much of what I write about is unrequited. SEPTEMBER 1983

It's funny that most people that get enchained to the idea of absolute love are usually totally irresponsible and self-deprecating individuals. SEPTEMBER 1983

I don't feel any relationship can be everlasting but something quite brief is manageable. 1984

Have you always denied love in the past?

Yes, always. I don't know why. It seemed safer. 1984

People need their bonds. DECEMBER 1984

I do know people who have no money, marry and live in very threadbare conditions and have threadbare requirements. I'm glad I'm no longer in that situation myself. DECEMBER 1984

No, I was being absolutely serious. Which isn't really funny. MARCH 1985

Were you being flippant when you said that your love songs were written from total guesswork?

If we're talking about romance, well, I don't really know that much about it. MARCH 1985

'Girl Afraid' simply implied that within relationships, there's no real certainty and nobody knows how anybody feels. People feel that simply because they're having this cemented communion with another person that the two of them will become whole, which is something I detested. I hate that implication. It's not true, anyway. Ultimately, you're on your own, whatever happens in life. MARCH 1985

Being in love is something I would never claim to fully understand. JUNE 1985

I am constantly in that state of desire and admiration for things, words . . . JUNE 1985

Have you ever fallen in love?

Yes, no, yes, no, yes, no . . . and that's about as clear as I can be. JUNE 1986

This word 'love' – people can quite easily say that they love marmalade or they love mushrooms, or they love people. JUNE 1985

I'm convinced that once it happens, if indeed it ever does, there will be a tremendous turnabout in my life and that's captivating and riveting to me. I'm waiting for it to happen. JUNE 1985

SMITHS

I think what The Smiths are is something quite beyond popular music, which could almost sound like an absurdly brash comment but it really is the truth. I think that's why I'm asked very serious questions. If we were simply blending in with modern popular music, we wouldn't be having this conversation.

FEBRUARY 1984

We want to make friends, we want to have people around us. Isn't that what everybody wants deep down? I'm sure when you were at school all you really cared about was being popular. All we care about is being popular and that's why we try hard to please. **NOVEMBER 1983**

When we started, inflated and elongated names were the order of the day. I wanted to explain to people that it wasn't necessary to have long names, dress in black and be po-faced. Our task was to choose the most ordinary of names and yet produce something of artistic merit. **NOVEMBER 1983**

We want to bring people back to earth, to open them up again. **NOVEMBER 1983**

I think of our music as a really passionate human cry. The main thing is to convince people that there's another train of thought that they can open up. I think people are generally afraid of emotionalism, and I want to change that. **NOVEMBER 1983**

People are dedicated to us because we deserve it. We try. Our reception hasn't surprised me at all. In fact, I think it will snowball even more dramatically over the immediate months – it really has to. I feel very comfortable about it, and I'm very pleased. It's all quite natural because I really think we merit a great deal of attention. **NOVEMBER 1983**

The Smiths is a very stray kind of name, very timeless. **MAY 1983**

We're out to prove that you don't need dazzling technology to produce music. There's a horrendous myth in modern music that you need the most complex equipment and the most far-reaching ideas, otherwise you don't rate. We've got back to a very traditionalist structure with the four-piece set-up which has been severely underrated in the past couple of years. **MAY 1983**

Control of artwork, etc., is of maximum importance. This is our product; we haven't come this far for some stranger to step in. We're not hollow musicians. **MAY 1983**

I wouldn't want The Smiths to be considered to be in any particular category. **SEPTEMBER 1983**

What is important is that we have a conviction that is quite rare. We write songs that have good lyrics and everything we do and say, we mean. **SEPTEMBER 1983**

People cannot trivialise The Smiths and people cannot trivialise anything we do. **SEPTEMBER 1983**

I don't think I'll wilt quickly. We'll never be a flavour of the month, I think we're just a little bit too clever for that. **FEBRUARY 1984**

For the first time in too long a time, this is real music played by real people. The Smiths are absolutely real faces instead of the frills and the gloss and the pantomime popular music has become immersed in, as a matter of course. There is no human element in anything any more. And I think The Smiths reintroduce that quite firmly. There's no façade, and we're very open and we're simply there to be seen as real people. **MARCH 1984**

We've got cases full of songs. We're recording a second LP right away, not to keep ourselves in the public eye but because we've got these songs bursting out – and we like working. **MARCH 1984**

I think that what we did is quite revolutionary and historic. We didn't spend a penny on promotion; we didn't do a video; we didn't take up any advertising space – all the things the industry says you have to do to be successful. And I feel quite slighted that our achievement has been overlooked by the industry. **JUNE 1984**

The band and I are in daily contact. But I don't feel I have to gaze at their profiles or anything. They do get a bit jealous sometimes, and I won't deny that they're not ecstatic when yet another interview with me appears. **FEBRUARY 1984**

I think something still separates us from the rest of the clatter. Where words are concerned, I try to use lines that have not been used in the history of popular music before, and for that reason alone it separates us. I think our audience recognises that we are different. **FEBRUARY 1984**

There's absolute perfect harmony within the group, and as each day passes it becomes stronger, which is more important to me than anything else. I have no interest in solo success or individual spotlights. **NOVEMBER 1984**

We've done a lot of work this year and achieved a great deal, much more than we've been given credit for. It's been a most thrilling year, and as four individuals, we are closer than ever before. But I've been quite aware for a few months that many journalists were trying to prize Johnny and I apart in some way. We've weathered that and we've weathered the most difficult backlash. I feel we're quite impenetrable. **DECEMBER 1984**

I see The Smiths as very extreme, in very positive ways.
DECEMBER 1984

We never listen to everyone else. I think the only thing to do with advice is ignore it, because people will never understand the real you. **DECEMBER 1984**

No, I don't. They're in The Smiths. **SEPTEMBER 1984**

We've never deliberately set out to court controversy but I think it is quite natural we always will. The lyrics are intellectual and that's too rare in modern music. **DECEMBER 1984**

Joining The Smiths was like a purging for me – it's been like a life-raft. **DECEMBER 1984**

I don't do anything just to surprise people. I'm not thinking, 'Now, what will fox them next?' It's not a circus and I'm not some trapeze artist. I think The Smiths are an irregular group, regardless of what we do. **DECEMBER 1984**

Because it occurred to me that nobody could put any possible connotations on the name. It came at a time when group names were vastly important, biblical, monstrous and had a great deal to say. They were very long and were in themselves a lifestyle. I wanted to get rid of all that kind of rhetorical drivel and just say something incredibly basic. The Smiths just sounded to me quite . . . um . . . down to earth. **SEPTEMBER 1984**

If I said yes, it'd make them out to be incurable heavy metal addicts, which they're certainly not. They're quite sensitive people. But they are more traditional musicians than I am. They like to party as often as they can. **SEPTEMBER 1984**

We just didn't want to be associated with them, which sounds quite brutal, but we'd come a long way, nobody had helped, and we didn't want anyone like The Police to feel they had a hand in helping us. **1984**

That people should discard any notions of in-ness or hip-ness or cool-ness, and simply relax and be themselves, whatever that may be. Ninety per cent of immediate daily anxieties are futile. **1984**

The image The Smiths provokes is so strong. It does provoke absolute adoration or absolute murderous hatred. There are people out there, I know, who would like to disembowel me – just as there are people who would race towards me and smother me with kisses. **1984**

Do you have many friends?

Why did you call the band The Smiths?

Are the rest of The Smiths keener on the rock 'n' roll lifestyle than you?

On rejecting a support gig with The Police:

What is the message of The Smiths?

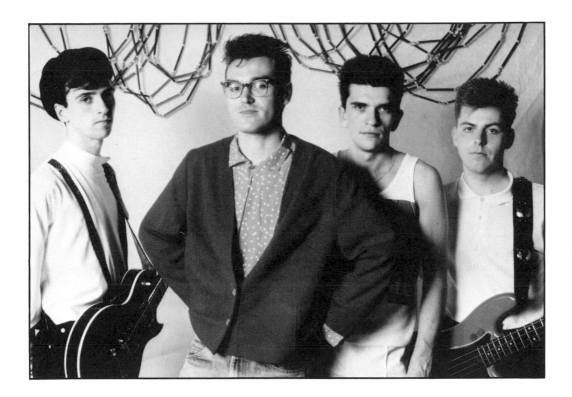

People want to throw a blanket over even the slightest mention of The Smiths, and the industry spends all its time denying that we're a phenomenon. I think it's because we have this grain of intellect, and when you as a band are trying to lay down the rules you're actually spoiling things for so many middle-aged mediocrities who control the whole sphere of popular music. Let me tell you, the music industry absolutely detests The Smiths. **MARCH 1985**

A lot of people say, 'You are big, you are heard, you do have your army of apostles – what are you complaining about?' But I'm in there every day, and I'm the one who knows that the profile we have on radio and television should be higher. But I still believe that The Smiths can become the most successful force in music. I think that would mean dramatic record sales – just unfathomably dramatic record sales – unbearable record sales. **AUGUST 1985**

There is a certain, shall we say, social standing that you have to take in to consume The Smiths without any degree of ruffled feathers. I think you have to be 'with it'. You have to be awake. You have to be up early. **1985**

Now that we have a big audience it's really important to me that people realise that we haven't become sloppy and we haven't become cushioned and we haven't become fat and lazy. Because we didn't want to go into the big league, as it were, and adhere to all the rules. That's pointless. It makes the entire history of The Smiths totally pointless. There has to be something that separates us. **MARCH 1985**

To be honest, we are very angry. We are angry about the music industry. We've very angry about pop music. **MARCH 1985**

When you become successful, people – if they've had even the vaguest connection with you – claim absolute responsibility for your success. But I can safely and honestly and loudly say that The Smiths have been successful without any help from a living soul anywhere on this planet. **JUNE 1985**

For a manager-less group like us to survive is miraculous. **JUNE 1985**

I really can't tolerate the trite attitude that's surrounded The Smiths signing to EMI. The concept that it's like getting into bed with Hitler is pathetic. **SEPTEMBER 1987**

The record industry regards The Smiths as a private concern; we exist in our own world, selling records to 'our' fans and no one else. Frankly, we've always suspected the records are simply abandoned as soon as they start dropping down the charts. There's also the logistical problem that because our fans trust The Smiths and buy our records immediately upon release, there are none left in the shops in week two. I'm just keeping everything crossed that none of these factors crop up with EMI or that's another theory gone west. **SEPTEMBER 1987**

The Smiths tease people – making them laugh, then making them cry – operating at opposite ends of the emotional scale. What we're ultimately hoping to do is to make them laugh and cry at the same time. **SEPTEMBER 1987**

We're always being advised to go abroad for 12 months to avoid all this awful, dreadful, nasty tax, but I couldn't go anywhere for 12 weeks, let alone 12 months, which is why The Smiths have never done a world tour. **SEPTEMBER 1987**

One of The Smiths' skills has been to take subjects which people might lazily presume are dark and morbid, and make them interesting, or turn them into the subjects of interesting songs. **SEPTEMBER 1987**

Neither Johnny nor I are compromisers which – plus the fact that we've never been prepared to do anything for money – means we've avoided many of the classic temptations of the whirlwind of pop. It's been relatively easy to sidestep all the glamour and gloss and the whole facetiousness of the pop industry. **SEPTEMBER 1987**

AMERICA

It's quite a good place if you belong and if you're not poor. But if you don't belong and if you are poor, I think it's the worst place in the universe. Obviously it's very materialistic and all of that — and it's a cultural wilderness, we all know that.

JUNE 1985

It's very important to me not to fall on to the rock 'n' roll treadmill. The very obvious thing that all groups do is to zip straight towards America. I want to go to America when we are wanted there. I'm very, very immersed in England and what's happening here, and I don't want to leave this country to work anywhere that might be utterly futile. JUNE 1984

America will be a challenge, it'll be interesting to see what they make of us over there. I don't think we fit into their idea of pop stars – thank goodness. SEPTEMBER 1984

In America it's really a terrible situation. Sire (The Smiths' US company) won't even acknowledge songs that have been successful here like 'Heaven Knows I'm Miserable Now' and 'William, It Was Really Nothing'. They won't put them on record in any conceivable form. To me that's a tremendous blow, an absolute insult. That makes me feel quite sad and inclined not to care that much about America. NOVEMBER 1984

How were you received in America?

It was very hysterical, very wild, very passionate, very moving. All those things people never believe. It was really quite stunning, even for me, to see it happen. AUGUST 1985

When you play concerts in America that are highly successful, it really colours your vision of the entire country. You're quite reluctant to think of the bad points because suddenly it seems like the most perfect patch of land on this planet. I've been there many times and had unshakeable criticisms which have now been shaken. AUGUST 1985

We went over there with quite a humble nature and we didn't expect any fanatical fervour or uncontrollable hysteria. So when it happened I was rendered speechless for months. AUGUST 1985

One is fed all these fixed impressions of the American record-buying public and they didn't turn out that way. They turned out to be rational, incredibly sensitive, poetic human beings. AUGUST 1985

I have relatives in America. I saved up the money when I was much younger – 17 – and went for the first time. I took this awful sickening job in this horrendous office in Manchester to save up the money. It was an Inland Revenue office; I was just filing and exciting things like that. 1985

I went on holiday to Los Angeles, which is in America. It was a silent holiday, a completely silent holiday. I went to a hotel, the hotel was empty. I never saw any people. It was like convalescing. I thought it would be exciting – Hollywood, all those famous stars . . . **1985**

Why is Reagan there? I'm sure this is a question that's even foxing Americans. It's the Daz mentality. I'm sure they'd elect Joan Collins if she was available. **JUNE 1985**

Taking on the whole of America single-handed – I'd need a lot of cornflakes to do that. **JUNE 1985**

I believe that everything went downhill from the moment the McDonald's chain was given licence to invade England – don't laugh I'm serious. To me it was like the outbreak of war and I couldn't understand why English troops weren't retaliating. The Americanisation of England is such a terminal illness – I think England should be English and Americans should go home and spoil their own country. **SEPTEMBER 1987**

ROYALTY

All the individuals within the Royal Family, they're so magnificently, unaccountably and unpardonably boring.

JUNE 1986

I despise royalty. I always have done. It's fairy story nonsense, the very idea of their existence in these days when people are dying daily because they don't have enough money to operate one radiator in the house; to me it's immoral. **MARCH 1985**

Money spent on royalty is money burnt. **MARCH 1985**

I've never met anyone who supports royalty, and believe me I've searched. OK, so there's some deaf and elderly pensioner in Hartlepool who has pictures of Prince Edward pinned on the toilet seat, but I know streams of people who can't wait to get rid of them. **MARCH 1985**

To me there's something dramatically ugly about a person who can wear a dress for £6,000 when at the same time there are people who can't afford to eat. When she puts on that dress for £6,000 the statement she is making to the nation is: 'I am the fantastically gifted royalty, and you are the snivelling peasants.' The very idea that people would be interested in the facts about this dress is massively insulting to the human race. **MARCH 1985**

The writers and designers of *Spitting Image* should be unmercifully sued for making the Royal Family seem generally more attractive and intelligent than they actually are. **1985**

I couldn't believe the number of people outside the palace on the Queen Mother's birthday. If the woman had died there would have been less. And I'd have been hammering the nails in the coffin to make sure she was in there. **1985**

I didn't want to attack the monarchy in a sort of beer monster way. But I find as time goes by this happiness we had slowly slips away and is replaced by something that is wholly grey and wholly saddening. The very idea of the monarchy and the Queen of England is being reinforced and made to seem more useful than it really is. **JUNE 1986**

It's disgusting, when you consider what minimal contribution they make in helping people. They never under any circumstances make a useful statement about the world or people's lives. The whole thing seems like a joke, a hideous joke. We don't believe in leprechauns so why should we believe in the Queen? **JUNE 1986**

The establishment – the monarchy and the government – don't care as far as I can see. Many of them are of advanced years but they do nothing for old people. **JUNE 1986**

69

Diana herself has never uttered one statement that has been of any use to any member of the human race. If we have to put up with these ugly individuals, why can't they at least do something off the mark. JUNE 1986

The royals are so staid and uninteresting. JUNE 1986

MEAT

We get violently upset when animals eat human beings. So why shouldn't we feel horror when human beings eat animals?

JANUARY 1985

Meat is murder. 1984

It is a direct statement. Of all the political topics to be scrutinised, people are still disturbingly vague about the treatment of animals. People still seem to believe that meat is a particular substance not at all connected to animals playing in the field over there. People don't realise how gruesomely and frighteningly the animal gets to the plate. **DECEMBER 1984**

Boots have a record in the country for testing out products on animals, murdering all these animals every single day. These people have to be attacked because they won't recognise communication between the Animal Liberation Front and themselves. Boycott Boots. **DECEMBER 1984**

I don't stand on the table and say you can't possibly eat that piece of meat, and go into a long monologue about it. I don't try and inflict the way I feel upon other people because that's quite boring. People know what meat is. **SEPTEMBER 1984**

Can you remember the last time you ate meat?

I can't really, but I didn't like it the last time. I'm quite sure it was bacon because I had a moderate bacon fetish. And I can remember as I came to the end of my bacon period, I thought: 'Oh, I don't like the taste of this any more.' It was simply the realisation of the horrific treatment of animals; I had never been aware of it before. I suppose I knew vaguely that animals died, but I didn't know how and I didn't know why. **JANUARY 1985**

Do you approve of the Animal Liberation Front?

Completely. I think we have to take these measures now because polite demonstration is pointless. You have to get angry, you have to get violent, otherwise what's the point? There's no point in demonstrating if you don't get any national press, TV or radio. So I do believe in these animal groups, but I think they should be more forceful and I think what they need now is a national figure, some very forthright figurehead. **JANUARY 1985**

I can't think of any reason why vegetarians should be considered effeminate. Why? Because you care about animals? Is that effeminate? Is that a weak trait? It shouldn't be, and I think it's a very sad reflection on the human race that it often is. **JANUARY 1985**

If I bought a pet today, I'd feed it on non-meat products like Smarties and baked beans. Animals can live without meat. **JANUARY 1985**

Violence towards animals, I think, is also linked to war. As long as human beings are so violent towards animals there will be war. It might sound absurd, but if you really think about the situation it all makes sense. Where there's this absolute lack of sensitivity where life is concerned, there will always be war. **MARCH 1985**

I feel animal rights groups aren't making any dramatic headway because most of their methods are quite peaceable. The only way we can get rid of the meat industry, and other things like nuclear weapons, is by really giving people a taste of their own medicine. **MARCH 1985**

HEROES AND VILLIANS

As for Oscar Wilde, his dandy style was greatly ridiculed, but I can't think of anything he wrote that doesn't move me. The idea of him always walking around with a flower appeals to me.

MARCH 1984

Sandie Shaw

SANDIE SHAW

Without supernatural beauty, Sandie Shaw cut an unusual figure, and would herald a new abandoned casualness for female singers. The *grande dame* gestures of the late fifties had gone, the overblown icky sentiment had gone, and in its place came a brashness and fortitude: girls with extreme youth and high spirits who were to boldly claim their patch in a business which was obviously a male domain. **DECEMBER 1983**

Working with her has been an endless thrill, it's almost like meeting oneself in a former life. She's very down to earth, very humorous, there's a certain veil which she lowers at a particular time of the day. **FEBRUARY 1984**

To me, working with Sandie was revolutionary. It proved to me that the gap between artists is really quite slim. The tabloids leapt on the case with great vigour. They were completely sceptical. 'Sandie, how can you possibly work with these blimps, these obscure characters from criminal areas of Manchester? How can you possibly soil your slippers?' So it was horror all round. We think that society is dedicated to the class system, but it's rife throughout the music industry. **FEBRUARY 1984**

On the face of it, the Sandie project was a tremendous success. I felt, at that time, that what we were doing was the absolute envy of the entire industry. It was The Smiths, these relative newcomers, and Sandie Shaw at the other extreme. Just the way we came together, the combination was almost perfect: it had virtually never been done before in the history of music. **DECEMBER 1984**

What did you say in your first love letter to Sandie?

It was incredibly well written and incredibly intelligent, quite short and blunt and to the point – I adore you, and when can we marry? Of course, there was no reply. **1984**

Our first contact was arranged by a mutual friend. I was shuffled round to her flat and there she was in pyjamas, holding her baby. It was very romantic. To me it was like a candle-lit dinner. What do I think of her? I think she'll do. **1984**

Our relationship is terribly private. In the press she tries to play it down, makes me out to be a deranged schoolboy. But in private I'm more like the deranged teacher. **1984**

OSCAR WILDE

My mother, who's an assistant librarian, introduced me to his writing when I was eight. She insisted I read him and I immediately became obsessed. I liked the simplicity of the way he wrote. He had a life that was really tragic and it's curious that he was so witty. **JUNE 1984**

'The artist must educate the critic.' Because it's true. The artist should be up above the critic. The critic should be a fan after all. **MARCH 1984**

What's your favourite Oscar Wilde saying?

Oscar Wilde and James Dean were the only two companions I had as a distraught teenager. Every line that Wilde ever wrote affected me so enormously. **JUNE 1984**

It's a total disadvantage to care about Oscar Wilde, certainly when you come from a working-class background. It's total self-destruction, almost. **JUNE 1984**

As I blundered through my late teens, I was quite isolated and Oscar Wilde meant much more to me. In a way he became a companion. If that sounds pitiful, that was the way it was. **JUNE 1984**

As I became a Smith, I used flowers because Oscar Wilde always used flowers. **JUNE 1984**

Oscar Wilde

As I get older the adoration increases. I'm never without him. It's almost biblical. It's like carrying your rosary around with you. **JUNE 1984**

He was a hideously fat person so I'm sure he indulged in meat quite often; but he is forgiven. **JANUARY 1985**

JAMES DEAN

I never thought much about his acting abilities, but the aura around him always fascinated me. When I mention James Dean to people they seem disappointed because it seems such a standard thing for a young person to be interested in – but I really can't help it. **NOVEMBER 1984**

I saw *Rebel Without A Cause* quite by accident when I was about six. I was entirely enveloped. I did research about him and it was like unearthing Tutankhamen's tomb. His entire life seemed so magnificently perfect. **JUNE 1984**

James Dean

At school it was an absolute drawback because nobody really cared about him. If they did, it was only in a synthetic rock 'n' roll way. Nobody had a passion for him as I did, for that constant uneasiness with life. That kind of mystical knowledge that there is something incredibly black around the corner. People who feel this are quite special and always end up in quite a mangled mess. JUNE 1984

I would like to go to Indiana and mess with James Dean's soil, but so many others have done it. They've taken away the monument, they've taken away the stone and they've taken away the grass. People have been so greedy. What's left for me? JUNE 1985

Thomas Hardy

New York Dolls

Lloyd Cole

THE REST

I'm moved by certain books rather than people. I can mention books by certain people that have set me alight. For instance, Thomas Hardy's *Far From The Madding Crowd* set me alight, but *The Mayor Of Casterbridge* didn't. And I feel that about so many people that I've liked, apart from perhaps Shelagh Delaney. **FEBRUARY 1984**

I've never made any secret of the fact that at least 50 per cent of my writing can be blamed on Shelagh Delaney who wrote *A Taste Of Honey*. **JUNE 1986**

Billy's singles are totally treasurable. I get quite passionate about the vocal melodies and the orchestration always sweeps me away. He always had such profound passion. **JUNE 1984**

I always liked The New York Dolls because they seemed like the kind of group the industry couldn't wait to get rid of. And that pleased me tremendously. I mean there wasn't anybody around then with any dangerous qualities so I welcomed them completely. Sadly, their solo permutations simply crushed whatever image I had of them as individuals. Now I think they're absolute stenchers. **NOVEMBER 1984**

I found meeting Billy Mackenzie was very erratic, quite indescribable. He was like a whirlwind. He simply swept into the place and he seemed to be instantly all over the room. It was a fascinating study but one, I think, that would make me dizzy if it happened too often. **NOVEMBER 1984**

Lloyd Cole is a tremendously nice person, much more fascinating than anything he's ever put on vinyl. I think he's a lovely person. **NOVEMBER 1984**

For me one of the greatest lyricists of all time is George Formby. His more obscure songs are so hilarious, the language was so flat and Lancastrian and always focused on domestic things. Not academically funny, not witty, just morosely humorous, and that really appeals to me. **DECEMBER 1984**

Billy Fury is virtually the same as James Dean. He was entirely doomed too, and I find that quite affectionate. **JUNE 1984**

Pat Phoenix

Frankie Goes To Hollywood

Are you aware of Green's press campaign against you?

On Bob Geldof's publicised hatred of him:

Pat Phoenix was simply a blizzard of professionalism – of goodwill, of warmth. She was like a hurricane. She simply exploded into the room and I was quite taken aback by this. You simply wanted to rush towards her bosom and remain there forever. **AUGUST 1985**

I was fascinated with the fact that Pete Burns was quite obviously despised by the music industry. And I felt a great affinity with that situation. Pete has been much maligned and he has a reputation for being difficult and arrogant. And in reality, he's one of the holiest saints that ever walked the earth. He's a living angel. **AUGUST 1985**

If a character like Pete Burns existed within classical music it would be a world revelation, but because he doesn't, he's just there and he's very silly and he's very funny and he's very entertaining and ultimately he doesn't mean anything. I think he's a wonderful person. **MARCH 1985**

People who achieve things artistically after persistent public floggings, after being roasted alive by the critics and after having doors slammed in their faces, interest me when they come out on top, smiling, in control, impregnable. That to me is treasurable. **JUNE 1985**

As individuals, Frankie Goes To Hollywood seem to have no interest or control. They've been peddled in much the same way as groups in the sixties were peddled. Their entire career has been orchestrated by unseen faces. **NOVEMBER 1984**

Albert Finney was the Northern boy made good which is why I can relate to him. I find that mood of a Northern person going to London and then returning home very poignant. The beauty of Finney was his natural quality as an actor. Even when I'm asleep I can't look natural. **JUNE 1986**

I couldn't fail to be aware of it because it appeared in almost every publication across the world. I thought everything he said had the stench of fear about it. **NOVEMBER 1984**

I was asked to contribute to the artists for animals record, but considering the other people involved – working with Limahl would be artistically and aesthetically wrong. **NOVEMBER 1984**

He said it on the radio the other day and it was totally unprovoked. It was as if he was quite anxious and desperate to put me down. The fact that Bob Geldof – this apostle, this religious figure who's saving all these people all over the globe – the fact that he can make those statements about me yet he seems protected, seems totally unfair. **MARCH 1985**

I'm bored stiff with them. JUNE 1985

Reggae to me is the most racist music in the entire world. It's an absolute glorification of black supremacy. SEPTEMBER 1986

The whole implication was to save these people in Ethiopia, but who were they asking to save them? Some 13-year-old girl in Wigan. People like Thatcher and the royals could solve the Ethiopian problem within 10 seconds. But Band Aid shied away from saying that – for heaven's sake, it was almost directly aimed at unemployed people. MARCH 1985

Band Aid is the undiscussable, I'm afraid. JANUARY 1985

Nobody younger than Bob Geldof was allowed near the stage because otherwise The Boomtown Rats would have seemed like a collection of brontosauri. JUNE 1986

I heard George Michael's 'I Want Your Sex' quite recently in the car. I wasn't deeply impressed. I thought it sounded like Ponce, I mean Prince. 1985

Madonna reinforces everything absurd and offensive. Desperate womanhood. Madonna is closer to organised prostitution than anything else. JUNE 1986

Madonna

For me Prince conveys nothing. The fact that he's successful in America is interesting simply because he's mildly fey and that hasn't happened before there. Boy George, again I think he really doesn't say anything either. JUNE 1986

If Prince came from Wigan he would have been slaughtered by now. OCTOBER 1986

I detest Stevie Wonder. SEPTEMBER 1986

I think Diana Ross is awful. SEPTEMBER 1986

I hate all those records in the Top 40 – Janet Jackson, Whitney Houston. I think they're vile in the extreme. SEPTEMBER 1986

Is it possible to have one? Well, if I'm horribly tortured and flogged to admit it . . . I think I'd rather face further flogging. 1984

Obviously to get on *Top Of The Pops* these days one has to be, by law, black. I think something political has happened and there has been a hefty pushing of all these black artists and all this discofied nonsense into the Top 40. SEPTEMBER 1986

FUTURE

When people see us as simply grinding out sausages, as it were, we'll have the sense to take a swift exit. I don't want to bore people, so if I thought The Smiths were an absolute hindrance to the human race then we'd break up.

FEBRUARY 1984

**How do you see yourself
in 20 years' time?**

I'll be a mildly amusing eccentric pottering around somewhere. I'll probably be finished with the music business and running a little second-hand bookshop with only my budgie for company. **SEPTEMBER 1984**

The traditional ambitions within music, we don't have them. I mean, going to Yugoslavia, to America, touring the world – that doesn't appeal to us in any small degree. **SEPTEMBER 1984**

I can see that we could attain the status of groups like Culture Club, but we absolutely refuse to do that. It's impossible for me to imagine The Smiths not being great, of sliding into a kind of pampered despair. To me The Smiths are great by definition. Once they stop being great they'll cease to exist. **NOVEMBER 1984**

I don't see that The Smiths have got to change, it's just not necessary. I still feel that The Smiths have hardly begun, we've just scratched the surface. We'll last for a very long time. **DECEMBER 1984**

I don't mind how I'm remembered so long as they're precious recollections. I don't want to be remembered for being a silly, prancing, nonsensical village idiot. But I really do want to be remembered. I want some grain of immortality. I think it's been deserved. It's been earned. **MARCH 1985**

Yes, but it seems unavoidable really. It seems totally unavoidable. **1985**

**Don't you worry you'll end
up 55 and all alone?**

I expect when the dust has settled after 'Strangeways' there will have to be some degree of rethinking, because we can't go on forever in our present form. Inevitably certain aspects of the band would become tarnished, so a slight readjustment will have to be made. I think now is absolutely the right time to do it. When something becomes too easy and it's all laid out for you, one is robbed of the joy of achievement. When there's no need to fight any more, it'll be time to pull up the shutters on The Smiths. **SEPTEMBER 1987**

I don't think EMI have anything to worry about – we're not planning anything drastic or supernatural. **SEPTEMBER 1987**

I don't want to walk on-stage with a hair transplant with shoes on the wrong feet. I find pop senility totally appalling to witness. I don't want to haul the carcass across the studio floor and reach for the bathchair as I put down the vocal. **FEBRUARY 1988**

LYRICS

The songs are personal — they're there to be discovered. The words are basic because I don't want anyone to miss what I'm saying. Lyrics that are intellectual or obscure are no use whatsoever.

SEPTEMBER 1983

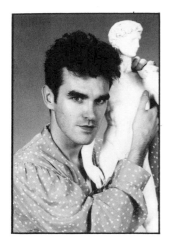

My lyrics are only obscure to the extent that they are not taken directly from the dictionary of writing songs. They are not slavish to the lyrical rule book so you'll never catch me singing, 'Oh baby, baby yeah.' My only priority is to use lines and words in a way that hasn't been heard before. **NOVEMBER 1983**

Reasons for writing aren't something I think about much, really. I've done it for such a long time now that to question it really seems quite ludicrous. It's like saying, 'Why do you breathe?' **NOVEMBER 1983**

The lyrics I write are specifically genderless. I don't want to leave anybody out. **MAY 1983**

I write strongly and I write very openly from the heart, which is something people aren't really used to. They're used to a very strict, regimented style – and if you dare to get too personal, and I don't mean offensively personal but just too close, then it's, 'What a strange person, let's get him on the guillotine.' **SEPTEMBER 1983**

I write persistently – it started when I was about two and leapt upon a typewriter. The rest is history. I feel people are just waiting for someone to say something and I've got a great deal to say. **NOVEMBER 1983**

I never intended to write the same song all the time, I do want some kind of variation, but nothing extreme. **FEBRUARY 1984**

I always find that the most powerful words are the most fundamental ones. It was always important to me to use lines that hadn't been said before, because it wasn't enough to use the usual pop terminology. **FEBRUARY 1984**

I could never use words that rhymed in a very traditional way. It would become absolutely pointless. So everything I write is very important to me. **MARCH 1984**

What I set out to do is to consider the sort of things people find difficult to say in everyday life. I don't think to say anything strong you have to burst into tears or to leap off the PA system. I thought you could just use a very natural voice, and say, this is what I feel, this is what I want, this is what I'm thinking about. **NOVEMBER 1984**

Language consists almost entirely of fashionable slang these days, therefore when somebody says something very blunt lyrically it's the height of modern revolution. **NOVEMBER 1984**

Something I abhor in modern music is the 'I' syndrome – 'I' did this, 'I' went here, 'I' did that. Well, I hate that and try to avoid 'I' as much as possible. But I still like the idea of songs being virtual conversation pieces – 'Tell me, why is your life like this?' I like the idea of being the sympathetic vicar. **DECEMBER 1984**

When I wrote 'That Joke Isn't Funny Anymore', I was just so completely tired of all the same old journalistic questions and people trying, you know, this contest of wit, trying to drag me down and prove that I was a complete fake. **MARCH 1985**

If anything, writing has become more important for me than ever. As a writer and lyricist I think I improve hourly – a lot of people say the first surge of Smiths' records were the best, but I really, really disagree. I make sure I write something every day and my flat is strewn with the debris of lyrics, finished and unfinished. **SEPTEMBER 1987**

I get ideas from almost everywhere but especially from supermarket queues – I have a talent for eavesdropping and it's amazing what you learn while waiting to pay for your fruit juice. **SEPTEMBER 1987**

I often wonder if we shouldn't explain ourselves more, especially as an astonishing number of people completely misunderstand The Smiths' humour. Take 'Bigmouth': I would call it a parody if that sounded less like self-celebration, which it definitely wasn't. It was just a really funny song. **SEPTEMBER 1987**

RECORDS

I really do expect the highest critical praise for the album ('The Smiths'). I think it's a complete signal post in the history of popular music.

FEBRUARY 1984

On the 'New York Mix' of
'This Charming Man':

I'm still very upset about that. It was entirely against our principles, the whole thing, it didn't seem to belong with us. There was even a question of a fourth version, which would have bordered on pantomime. It was called the Acton version, which isn't even funny. **FEBRUARY 1984**

A good portion of our mail contains imploring demands that we release versions of our songs that we recorded for Radio One sessions, and the band and I suddenly realised that we hadn't even proper-sounding tapes of them ourselves, except for a few dire bootlegs that we bought at our concerts.
As far as we're concerned, those were the sessions that got us excited in the first place, and apparently it was how a lot of other people discovered us also. We decided to include the extra tracks from our 12" singles for people who didn't have all of those, and to make it completely affordable. **OCTOBER 1984**

'Meat Is Murder' got to number one.

Yes it did, but its lifespan was embarrassingly short. And the amount of media attention that that LP had was extraordinary. Yet it really couldn't hold on. It dropped from the national 100 after 13 weeks. But 'Shakespeare's Sister', regardless of what many people feel, was the song of my life. I put everything into that song and I wanted it more than anything else to be a huge success, and – as it happens – it wasn't. **AUGUST 1985**

The whole idea with 'Meat Is Murder' was to control it totally, and without a producer things were better. We saw things clearer. **MARCH 1985**

On 'Meat Is Murder':

I didn't really have any intention of being misunderstood with the words on this LP. A lot of people wrote about the first LP and they said things that were very poetic and interesting and absolutely inaccurate. So I just felt that on this LP people should really know which hammer I'm trying to nail, as it were. **MARCH 1985**

Why is the new album called 'Strangeways Here We Come'?

Because the way things are going, I wouldn't be surprised if I was in prison 12 months from now. Really it's me throwing both arms up to the skies and yelling, 'Whatever next?' I don't have any particular crimes in mind but it's so easy to be a criminal nowadays that I wouldn't have to look very far. **SEPTEMBER 1987**

'Strangeways' perfects every lyrical and musical notion The Smiths have ever had. It isn't dramatically, obsessively different in any way, and I'm quite glad it isn't, because I'm happy with the structure we've had until now. It's far and away the best record we've ever made. **SEPTEMBER 1987**

On 'Hatful Of Hollow':

We wanted it released on purely selfish terms because we liked all those tracks and those versions. I wanted to present those songs again in the most flattering form. Those sessions almost caught the very heart of what we did – there was something positively messy about them. People are so nervous and desperate when they do those sessions, so it seems to bring out the best in them.
DECEMBER 1984

On 'Viva Hate':

Times are different and my life has moved on since The Smiths in very specific ways, and 'Viva Hate' is in no way the follow-up to 'Strangeways'. So in a sense I do feel that it is the first record.
MARCH 1988

Why 'Viva Hate'?

It simply suggested itself and had to be. It was absolutely how I felt post-Smiths and the way I continue to feel. That's just the way the world is. I find hate omnipresent and love very difficult to find. Hate makes the world go round. **MARCH 1988**

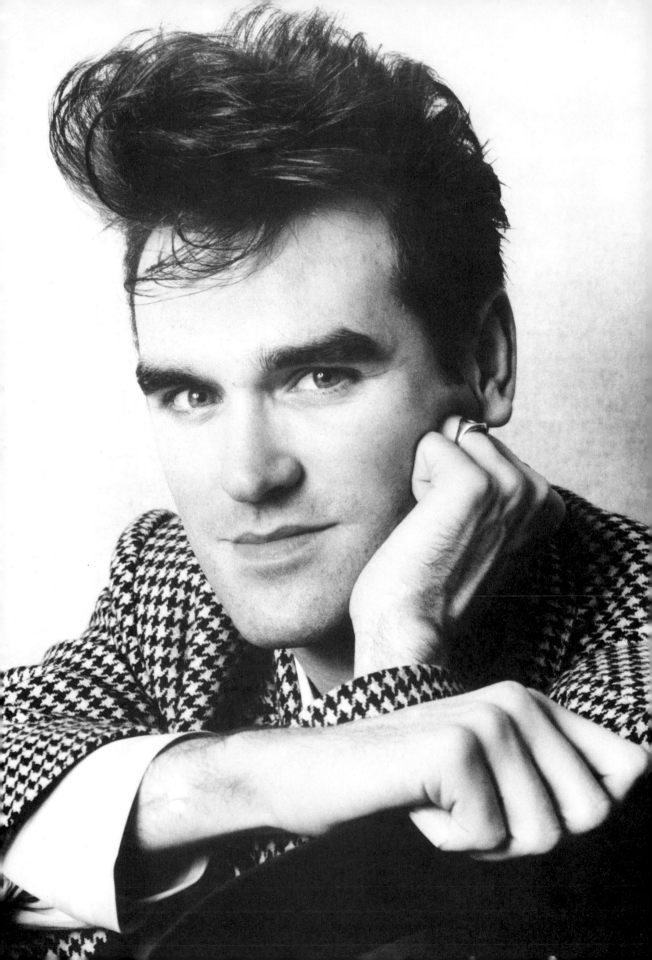

S P L I T

It's a very popular attitude that the split occurred at the right time. I get quite violent when people say that to me.

FEBRUARY 1988

The Smiths were almost like a painting: every month you'd add a little bit here and a little bit there; but it wasn't quite complete and it was whipped away. And I find it quite hard to adapt to that. Those people who patted me on the back and said, 'Oh! Smiths split! *Very* clever, *very* wise, *very* cunning' – I hadn't a clue what they were talking about. **FEBRUARY 1988**

Within The Smiths, the reason it worked so well was that everybody knew their place and their capabilities and each other's position. It was such a tight unit, and nobody it seemed could penetrate The Smiths' little secret private world. On the occasion that somebody did break through the mould, everything fell in 25 different directions. **FEBRUARY 1988**

Stephen Street had been working with The Smiths since 'Heaven Knows I'm Miserable Now', quite a long time ago. So Stephen's relationship with The Smiths as a group was totally harmonious and very natural. There was no undercurrent of awkwardness at all. As far as writing with Stephen is concerned, he sent me a tape in late August. It was the last thing on earth I expected. He simply sent a tape of his songs and said, 'Would you like to go in and record these?' He was very shy about it. **FEBRUARY 1988**

Although there's no pleasure for me in smearing Rough Trade – I can see their dilemmas and I understand them – I simply feel that, in the final analysis, The Smiths were not looked upon as the little treasures that they actually were. I certainly feel that I was the only group member who was ever treated with any respect. **FEBRUARY 1988**

We were being treated like some untried independent group from Harrogate and it was not acknowledged at all, in the Rough Trade network, that we were saving their skins. **FEBRUARY 1988**

I would be totally in favour of a reunion – which isn't to cast doubts on the album or the immediate future. If a reunion never occurs I'm sure I'll be quite happy as I am. But yes, I do entertain those thoughts, and as soon as anybody wants to come back to the fold and make records, I will be there! **FEBRUARY 1988**

I expect it's hard to believe that there weren't some elements of hatred slipping in and out. But it became a situation where people around the band began to take sides, and there was even a belief that within the audience there was a Morrissey contingent and a Marr contingent. And critics began to separate, and praise one and

On Johnny Marr

On the first solo Radio
One session

Have you made any
plans?

condemn the other. I *personally* did not find this a strain. But I find acrimony and even dwelling on the final events very futile. **MARCH 1988**

Because there were so many people around the group, everyone had their own exaggerations, and stories began to breed. **MARCH 1988**

The Smiths never earned *any* money touring. We'd come off remarkably successful tours and have to sit down and sign 80 cheques. It got *totally* out of control. This, if anything, was the cause of The Smiths' death. Especially the monetary side. We were making huge amounts of money and it was going everywhere but in the personal bank accounts of the four group members. And finally, I think, Johnny had to back off from that and put his entire life into the hands of his manager, because there was too much pressure. **MARCH 1988**

I haven't heard anything about him or of him since a year ago. The last time The Smiths were together was May 21, 1962, or whenever it was, which was a year ago. So since then I haven't heard a dickie bird, as they say. **JUNE 1988**

It was really awful, horrible. The engineers are quite accustomed to treating everyone like they were some insignificant, unsigned group from Poole. And that's how I felt on that day. I felt as though I'd never seen a record, let alone made one. So I found them a bit rude and I couldn't sing because I was so annoyed and angry. I think John Walters made a reference to it, saying I just didn't want it aired because I didn't think it was good enough, but the reason behind it was the situation at Maida Vale studio. **JUNE 1988**

There is no controversy on 'Viva Hate' as far as I can see, apart perhaps from the title. But I've never been deliberately controversial. It just so happens that because of the climate and the standards of writing in pop music today that if one has any self judgement about the things that you write, then you're bound to be considered not controversial, but at least . . . I've forgotten the word . . . Tesco's! **JUNE 1988**

None whatsoever. **JUNE 1988**

One way or another, I will always be *somewhere* just skating about the edges of global fame, pestering people and throwing glasses. **FEBRUARY 1988**